E. W Whitaker

Family Sermons

Volume 3

E. W Whitaker

Family Sermons
Volume 3

ISBN/EAN: 9783337161002

Printed in Europe, USA, Canada, Australia, Japan

Cover: Foto ©Lupo / pixelio.de

More available books at **www.hansebooks.com**

FAMILY SERMONS.

BY THE

REV. E. W. WHITAKER,

LATE OF CHRIST CHURCH, OXFORD:

NOW RECTOR OF ST. MILDRED'S AND ALL SAINTS, CANTERBURY.

VOL. III.

" FEED MY SHEEP."

LONDON:

PRINTED BY BYE AND LAW;

AND SOLD BY

F. AND C. RIVINGTON,

NO. 62, ST. PAUL'S CHURCH YARD.

1799.

ADVERTISEMENT

TO THE

THIRD VOLUME.

―――

SINCE from the uncertainty of the time at which the courfe may be entered on by different readers, it was impoffible the four occafional Sermons on the Spring, the Harveft, the Nativity, and the Crucifixion, fhould be properly placed in it, they are inferted before the concluding Difcourfe, that the reader may turn to and introduce them at the proper feafon, without further interrupting the general line. For the Authour has to requeft, that, as the whole courfe was compofed with a view to its being regularly gone through, his readers would, not only in juftice to the work, but for the purpofe of rendering the contents of it more

ADVERTISEMENT.

easy to be understood and retained, take that mode of reading it, in lieu of selecting each Sunday that Discourse which may strike the idea of the moment.

On reviewing the List of Subscribers, the Authour suspects there are some mistakes, but as he is not perfectly acquainted with the names and designation of those to whom he has not the honour of being personally known, he could only copy them as they stood in the lists made out at the booksellers, which he has faithfully done, and trusts, this will plead for his pardon with any one who may be improperly designated.

A LIST

OF THE

SUBSCRIBERS.

A.

LADY ARDEN, the Rolls.

B.

William Baker, Esq; M. P. Herts.
Mrs. Baker.
Mr. Baker, Salt Office.
Mrs. Barclay.
Mrs. Bennet, Rohamstead, Herts.
Rev. J. L. Bennett, Thorpe, Surrey.
Thomas Bennett, Esq; Upper Brook Street.
Mrs. George Berkeley, Thames Bank House, Henley
Mr. Berry, Mount Street.
J. F. Blach, Esq; Homerton, Middlesex.
Sir Edward Blackett, Bart. Thorpe Lee, Surrey.
Rev. H. Blackett, Balden, Durham.
William Bleamire, Esq; Highbury Place, Islington
Edmund Boehm, Esq; Ottershaw, Chertsey, Surrey.

SUBSCRIBERS.

Rev. Mr. Boucher, Vicar of Epsom, Surrey.
—— Bouchier, Esq; Sundridge Lodge, Herts.
George Bristow, Esq; Merchant Taylor's Hall.
Robert Bristow, Esq; Spring Gardens.
Rev. William Browne, Camfield, Herts.
Mrs. B. Browne.
Miss D. Browne.
William Bullock, Esq; Burstead, Essex, 2 copies.
Mr. Burton, Egham, Surrey.
Mr. S. Butler, Chertsey, Surrey.
Mrs. Buckworth, Old Windsor, Berks.

C.

Right Hon. Lady Camelford, 2 copies.
Hon. Frederick Cavendish, Market Street, Bedfordsh.
Mrs. Bromley Chester, Upper Brook Street.
Richard Clarke, Esq; Chamberlain of London.
Mrs. Clarke, Abbey Orchard, St. Alban's, Herts.
John Clarke, Esq; Sundridge Bury, Herts.
Rev. T. Cogan, Chichester.
Rev. James Cowe, Sunbury, Middlesex.

D.

Mr. William Davis, Trinity College, Cambridge.
Mrs. De Luc, Windsor, Berks.
Rev. William Dickins, Chervelton, Northamptonshire.

F.

Mrs. G. Firebrace, Dover, Kent.
Rev. Mr. Filkes, Woburn, Bedfordshire.

Rev.

SUBSCRIBERS.

Rev. Mr. Francis, Canterbury.
Mrs. W. Freemantle, Stanhope Street, May Fair.
Mr. Furnival, Egham, Surrey.

G.

Rev. Dr. Gaſkin, Rector of St. Bennet, &c.
Mr. R. Gates, Egham, Surrey.
George Gipps, Eſq; Canterbury.
Mrs. Gipps.
Mr. Gray, Highbury Place, Iſlington.
Rev. Mr. Green, Vice-Preſident of Magdalen College, Oxford.
Miſs Green, Great Ruſſel Street, Bloomſbury.
Rev. William Gregory, Canterbury.
Mr. Griffith, Fellow of Merton College, Oxford.
Sir William Guiſe, Bart.
Lady Guiſe.

H.

Thomas Hall, Eſq; Egham, Surrey.
—— Hamilton, Eſq; Old Windſor, Berks.
Mr. Harvey Watton, Norfolk.
Rev. John Hey, D. D.
Mrs. Heylin, Guildford Street.
Mrs. Hobhouſe, Briſtol.
T. Hobhouſe, Eſq; Temple.
John Hole, Eſq; Iſlington.

SUBSCRIBERS.

I.

Miss Jennings, Windsor Forest.
Rev. R. Ingram, Vicar of Wormingford and Boxted, Essex.
Mrs. Joddrel.
Mr. Johnson, Purly Place, Croydon.

K.

T. Kemble, Esq; Mark Lane.
Nathaniel Kent, Esq; Windsor Park.
E. King, Esq; Mansfield Street.

L.

Sir Soulden Lawrence, Knight, &c.
Sir Robert Lawrie, Bart. &c.
Lady Lawrie.
Mr. Lepine, Canterbury.
Rev. James Liptrot, Egham, Surrey.
Mr. C. P. Living, Chertsey, Surrey.
Mr. Lucas, Egham, Surrey.

M.

His Grace the Duke of Marlborough.
Her Grace the Duchess of Marlborough.
Barrett March, Esq.
Mr. March, Merchant Taylor's Hall.
Samuel Martin, Esq; Chertsey, Surrey.
Mrs. D. Monk.
George Monkland, Esq; Bath.

Lady

SUBSCRIBERS.

N.

Lady Neave, Albemarle Street.
Mr. Norris, Grove Street, Hackney, Middlesex.

O.

The Right Rev. the Bishop of Oxford.
Mrs. Ormsby.
Mrs. Owen, St. James's Place.

P.

Mrs. Parry, Warfield, Berks.
Mrs. Paulhan, Abbey Orchard, St. Alban's, Herts.
Rev. Mr. Pettingal, Easthamstead, Berks.
Mrs. Phipps, Highgate, Middlesex.
Mrs. Pocock, Egham, Surrey.
Rev. T. Preston, West Ham, Essex.

R.

John Rae, Esq; Ashford, Middlesex.
Joseph Revel, Esq; Egham, Surrey.
Mrs. Rochliff, Upper Brook Street.
—— Rofs, Esq; Upper Harley Street.
Rev. Mr. Ruffell, Bodians.

S.

Right Hon. Countess Dowager Spencer.
Spencer Schutz, Esq; Sunninghill, Berks.
Rev. B. L. Sclater, Ashford, Middlesex.
Mrs. Sclater.
Mrs. Scott, Thorpe, Surrey.
Mrs. Scott, Highgate, Middlesex.
Rev. T. Scott, Rector of King's Stanley, Gloucestersh.

Mrs.

SUBSCRIBERS.

J. M. Shaw, Esq; Ashford, Middlesex.
Mrs. Sibley, Maccary End, Herts.
William Smith, Esq; Egham, Surrey, 2 copies.
Mrs. Stanley, Egham, Surrey.
Mrs. Standerwick, Ovington, Hants.
Mr. John Stevens, Egham, Surrey.

T.

Right Hon. Lord Teignmouth.
Rev. Mr. Tate.
Mrs. Trimmer, Brentford, Middlesex.

Mr. Vansittart.
Mrs. Vansittart.

W.

Mr. Wallis, Bookseller, Ludgate Street.
Mrs. Wapshott, Egham, Surrey.
Rear Admiral West, Egham, Surrey.
Rev. C. White, Chertsey, Surrey.
William White, Esq; Highbury Place, Islington.
J. R. Whiteford, Esq; Egham, Surrey.
Mrs. Wright, Blakesley Hall.
John Wightwick, Esq; Sandgates, Chertsey, Surrey.
T. Wilson, Esq; Fenchurch Street.
R. Wilson, Esq; Berry Street.
A. Winterbottom, Esq; Threadneedle Street.
Mrs. Isabella Wyatt.
Richard Wyatt, Esq; Milton Place, Egham, Surrey, 2 copies.
E. Wyatt, Esq; Weymouth Street.

CONTENTS

OF THE

THIRD VOLUME.

SERMON I.
On Purity.

PETER ii. 11.

Dearly beloved, I beseech you as strangers and pilgrims, abstain from fleshly lusts, which war against the soul - - - - - 1

SERMON II.
On Theft and Fraud.

EPHES. IV. 28.

Let him that stole steal no more: but rather let him labour, working with his hands the thing which is good, that he may have to give to him that needeth 23

CONTENTS.

SERMON III.   Page

On the Government of the Tongue.

ST. MATT. XII. 36.

But I say unto you, that every idle word that men speak, they shall give account thereof in the day of judgment: for by thy words thou shalt be justified, and by thy words thou shalt be condemned - 45

SERMON IV.

On Covetousness.

EXOD. XX. 17.

Thou shalt not covet thy neighbour's house; thou shalt not covet thy neighbour's wife, nor his man-servant, nor his maid-servant, nor his ox, nor his ass, nor any thing that is thy neighbour's - - 65

SERMON V.

On the Love of our Neighbour.

ROM. XIII. 8.

Owe no man any thing, but to love one another: for he that loveth another hath fulfilled the law - 85

CONTENTS.

SERMON VI.
On the Lord's Supper.

I COR. XI. 26.

For as often as ye eat this bread, and drink this cup, ye do shew the Lord's death till He come - 105

SERMON VII.
On the last Judgement.

REV. XX. 12.

And I saw the dead, small and great, stand before God; and the books were opened: and another book was opened, which is the book of life: and the dead were judged out of those things which were written in the books, according to their works - 123

SERMON VIII.
On the same.

The same Text - - - - 147

SERMON IX.
On the same.

The same Text - - - - 165

CONTENTS.

SERMON X.
On the future State of Happiness.

REV. XXI. I.

And I saw a new heaven and a new earth - 185

SERMON XI.
On the future Punishment of the Wicked.

ST. MATT. XXV. 46.

And these shall go away into everlasting punishment 207

SERMON XII.
On the Tendency and Use of temporal Afflictions.

PSALM CXIX. 75.

I know, O Lord, that thy judgements are right, and that Thou in faithfulness hast afflicted me - 227

SERMON XIII.
On the Spring.

PSALM CIV. 14.

He causeth the grass to grow for the cattle, and herb for the service of man; that he may bring forth food out of the earth - - - 243

CONTENTS.

SERMON XIV.
On the Harvest.

GEN. VIII. 22.

While the earth remaineth, feed time and harvest, cold and heat, summer and winter, and day and night, shall not cease - - - - 263

SERMON XV.
On the Signs of the Times.

REV. III. 19.

As many as I love, I rebuke and chasten: be zealous, therefore, and repent - - - 281

SERMON XVI.
On the Nativity.

ST. LUKE ii. 11.

For unto you is born this day in the city of David a Saviour, which is Christ the Lord - - 305

CONTENTS.

SERMON XVII.

On the Crucifixion.

TIT. II. 14.

Who gave himself for us, that He might redeem us from all iniquity, and purify unto Himself a peculiar people, zealous of good works - - 325

SERMON XVIII.

Concluding Sermon.

ST. LUKE XII. 32.

Fear not, little flock, for it is your Father's good pleasure to give you the kingdom - - 343

SERMON I.

ON PURITY.

---

1 PETER II. 11.

Dearly beloved, I beseech you as strangers and pilgrims, abstain from fleshly lusts, which war against the soul.

IN the discourses lately read to you on the personal vices they have been considered, as they impel us to injure those connected with us in society; but since some who are unwilling to part with forbidden indulgences, deceive themselves by imagining, that they so manage their intemperance, as to hurt not their neighbours, and would persuade others of the harmlessness of their conduct; it is necessary further to reflect, whether compliance with any inordinate desire

desire does not naturally hurt the person guilty of it; and whether these desires do not, in the words of the text, war against the soul?

The character in which the apostle here considers Christians, supplies an argument for the conduct he has enjoined, which is by no means sufficiently attended to. Were men like the brutes that perish, designed only for this life, had they nothing farther to look to than this earthly habitation, admonitions against indulgence here could not justly be pressed beyond such restraint as is necessary to keep them from trespassing on others, or bringing temporal damage on themselves. But this being what might properly be termed a place of education for another state, in which our everlasting situation will be according to the spiritual improvement we have acquired here, and all who will not follow holiness being expresly debarred from entrance into the happiness and glories of the future life, it is evident, that to discover the measure of abstinence neces-

necessary here, we must consider, what neglect of it will operate to our exclusion from honour and felicity hereafter: and from the fact of our being only pilgrims and strangers on earth, manifestly arises the consequence of worldly desires and fleshly lusts warring against the soul.

Neither has this consequence, though not sufficiently regarded by some who reckon themselves among the faithful, been always overlooked by the more avowed patrons of vice; they have seen, that there is something which justice requires should be punished, in creatures to whom their Maker hath given understanding, and a consciousness that they ought to obey its dictates, acting in direct opposition to those dictates, and putting themselves under the sole government of their appetites. They have perceived, that evil consequences might be dreaded from a man's having his heart replete with foul desires, and his mind crowded with loose and impure images; and that the common sense of mankind will

will suggest a fear, that those who become slaves to their lusts, are laying up to themselves a stock of misery for the whole future duration of their existence. To counteract, therefore, the impression of these things on the human mind, they have propagated the doctrine, that no other state is to be expected after this, and endeavoured to make the multitude believe, that death is an eternal sleep.

And should not this acknowledgement alarm the Christian transgressor for the soundness of his reasoning, when he argues, that if he injure not others by it, the gratification of his appetites cannot bring him into condemnation? Should it not influence him to consider, what is the common ground on which an apostle of Christ declares, and the votaries of sin are induced to confess, that fleshly lusts war against the soul?

The effects of indulgence are sufficiently visible in the world, and human experience amply

amply proves the almost unconquerable power of habit. Observe to how disgraceful a state of impotence men are often reduced by the former of these; how incapable do they become of supporting, with decent fortitude, the least disappointment; by what trifling circumstances are they stung with vexation! What an absurd anxiety do they betray about things not worth a moment's care! and such is the debility of mind which they have contracted, that even from the enjoyment of their favourite objects, they receive but a peevish pleasure! and now consider, what a preparation is such a debilitated state of soul, such a contracted restlessness, and unsatisfied disposition for entrance into that heavenly society, of which we are taught the real followers of Christ shall be admitted members. But if indulgence in particulars, not criminal perhaps in themselves, which partake not of uncleanness, to which no impurity is attached, thus weakens the powers of the soul, What injury must she receive from practices, at the very commencement of which, her sense of right and wrong is forcibly opposed, and in the course of them her moral taste gradually vitiated by repeated submission to the lusts of the flesh! That carnal gratifications do in fact debase men's minds, turn them from noble pursuits, bias their reasonings, and obscure their understandings, a little attentive observation will convince you.

Mark to what meannesses some who in other respects manifest an high spirit, and are indeed men of great pride, will submit; with what companions they will disgrace themselves, to what insults they will stoop, of what dissimulation they will be guilty, when once enslaved by their inordinate desires. We see the most honourable pursuits given up, the noblest prospects in life relinquished, the closest connections broken off, and the nearest, and those which ought to be the dearest relatives, neglected, for the sake of undisturbed indulgence in some base gratification, of wallowing without inter-

interruption, like the fow in her mire. Yet did any man, think ye, ever begin his vicious courfe with intent to fubmit to fuch thraldom? No; having formed a plan of proceeding no further in tranfgreffion than, he abfurdly imagined, would, under his own particular circumftances, admit of excufe: thinking to continue under the reftraints of reafon practices which he commenced contrary to all reafon; he yielded to the dominion of paffion; and when he wanted to refume the command of himfelf, found he had made mafters of thofe he meant to be his flaves. Confcious of his degraded fituation, and fearing, or hurt, that others fhould remark it, his generous love of praife, and dread of difgrace, are contracted into a peevifh jealoufy left his character fhould be reflected on, and the native vigour of his mind is loft, fcarcely or never to be recovered.

Behold, then, how in this fenfe flefhly lufts war againft the foul, by bringing it into a bondage fo fevere, that although their victims

victims see the evil tendency of their own conduct, though they feel its bad effects on their reputation, their health, or their circumstances, though distress, poverty, and ruin, stare them in the face, unable to restrain desires, the great impetuosity of which arose from their being at first cherished, they are driven forward to the afflictions which they foresaw, only after they had deprived themselves of the power of preventing them. And must not minds thus enfeebled, souls thus debased, be hopeful candidates for glory in a future state, where our qualifications for an honourable station will be judged of by the fidelity we have shewn in using the powers entrusted to us here: and our fitness to have any thing of our own, by the use we have hitherto made of that which was another's? It is not, therefore, the present ease and honour of the soul only against which carnal appetites militate, but against her future dignity, her everlasting happiness.

To

To defcry, however, ftill more ample evidence of this, let us more accurately confider the habits contracted by thofe who are led away by inordinate defires, and the natural effects of thofe habits. We may take the inftance in any kind of wickednefs; the world will afford us examples of every fort. Obferve, then, a man who has yielded to the love of gain. See him not ceafing from his endeavours to accumulate, when he has acquired fufficient to provide himfelf during the longeft term of days for which he can hope in this world, not only the neceffaries and conveniences, but even the luxuries of life; but denying himfelf all thofe gratifications as the means of which only riches theirfelves are defirable: toiling day and night, undergoing labour of which his felf complains, to heap up wealth which he is confcious he can never enjoy: while neither the perpetual anxiety he fuffers, nor his fenfe of the contemptible figure he exhibits, nor his dread of the fearful judgments of Him who has by His apoftle declared, that covetoufnefs is idolatry,

try, can prevail on him to relinquish his habits of parsimony, or desist from the pursuit of lucre.

Or, turn your attention to the votaries of pleasure and dissipation; mark the force of the habits they have acquired; against which neither the admonitions of friendship, the ties of natural affection, the dread of want, nor the sanctions of religion, avail. Or, consider the situation of those whose wretched state calls still more loudly for observation, those, I mean, who abandon themselves to the most profligate pursuit of both pleasure and profit in the vice of gaming. Among these ye may see persons even of that sex whose more tender affections and delicate feelings would, we might suppose, revolt at plans of ruin and scenes of treachery, relinquish the domestick attachments, and become so hardened by custom, that neither the rebukes of those to whose words they are bound to listen, nor the calls of parental duty, nor remorse for contributing to pierce the hearts of others

others with affliction, nor even the publick indignation and contempt, can induce them to refrain from giving their honour unto others, and their years unto the cruel; from letting strangers be filled with their wealth; and the labours of their husbands or their ancestors be in the house of a stranger; until they mourn at the last, when their flesh and their bodies are consumed. But as the habits of vice are obstinate, so are their effects forcible: among the first of these may be ranked a disinclination to every better pursuit, a decrease of horrour at further degrees of guilt, and necessarily, a dislike to all moral instruction and all the truths of religion. Neither is this the utmost of their extent; for as the views of the soul are debased, so is the light of the understanding obscured; the quickness of the conception being blunted, and the soundness of the judgement vitiated. Hence the vain babblings of the profligate against the doctrines of the Gospel, the nonsensical arguments they run through to persuade themselves and others, that they may sin, and

no

no harm happen unto them: hence their contemptible credulity in the cafes of fo many falfe pretenders to knowledge; hence the readinefs with which they embrace the French philofophy; hence their diflike to the facred writings, their neglect of the affemblies of the church, and their averfion from hearing that they have fouls, which, indeed, are not in the road to falvation.

Thus doth fin block up every path to amendment, and obftruct every avenue to repentance fo completely, that though the Lord be conftantly working around them, thofe who yield themfelves in bondage to flefhly lufts cannot perceive Him, until He fpeak to them in thunder. The pure in heart only can fee God. It is no matter of furprife, therefore, if thofe whofe hearts are replete with foul imaginations, and whofe inclinations fet upon the low enjoyments of the earth, cannot comprehend how it fhould be His will that men fhould live foberly, righteoufly, and godly, or that none fhould partake of His falvation, or be admitted

admitted to His kingdom, who is not cleanfed from all iniquity. No wonder if thofe who can figure to themfelves no future happinefs for which it is worth while to abftain from the gratification of the bodily appetites at prefent, can form no idea of a ftate of perfect blifs, from whence all their favourite pleafures are banifhed. But it is manifeft, that if men of fuch habits were even admitted into the fociety of the bleffed above, far from deriving fatisfaction from the pure employments and fpiritual converfation of fuch, the holinefs of their companions would be a reproach unto them, and the abfence of every object in which they were accuftomed to find pleafure, would make Heaven itfelf no Heaven to them. And thus again, do flefhly lufts war againft the foul!

Having hitherto enquired how the lufts of the flefh war againft the foul by affecting its powers, rendering it unfit for the dignity and honours of a future ftate of glory, and incapable of participating in the
happi-

happiness of that heavenly kingdom, even were it admitted to an inheritance therein, let us consider, how they do the same by leading men to transgress the divine commandments.

That every kind of impurity, even that of thought, is forbidden by the Gospel, I need not go about to prove; nor that obedience to the laws of God is a specified condition of our attaining to the life of the world to come. Ye scarcely need be reminded of our blessed Lord's answer to him who asked, what good thing he should do, that he might have eternal life. " If thou wilt enter into life, keep the commandments:" or of His comparison of every one that heareth His sayings, and doeth them not, to a foolish man, who built his house upon the sand: neither of His apostle's declaration, which both states plainly what are the works of the flesh, and the penalty on doing them. " Now the works of the flesh are manifest, which are these; adultery, fornication, uncleanness, lasciviousness, oufnefs, idolatry, witchcraft, hatred, variance, emulations, wrath, ftrife, feditions, herefies, envyings, murders, drunkennefs, revellings, and fuch like; of the which I tell you before, as I have alfo told you in time paft, that they which do fuch things fhall not inherit the kingdom of God."

After denunciations fo plain and pofitive as thefe, whence can arife the abfurd imagination, that any thing lefs than fincerely breaking off our fin by repentance can prevent our being excluded from that glorious inheritance, unlefs it be from the pernicious fuggeftion of the fame tempter who faid unto the firft woman, when fhe urged the divine prohibition of eating from the tree of the knowledge of good and evil, " Ye fhall not furely die?" In liftening to this affurance of the father of lies, fhe daringly and ungratefully charged her Creatour and only Benefactor with unkindly laying a needlefs reftraint on the works of His own hands: and doth not every man who, either by word or action, denies the neceffity or import-

importance of the Gospel-precepts of purity, in like manner charge God foolishly? Does he not withdraw himself from the protection of his Maker, and madly signify, that he can look better to himself? Whether men will own it, whether they see it or not, this is in reality the declaration which they make when they knowingly transgress the divine commandments; and whether, after that, they will be admitted to partake in the divine promises, or be delivered from the wrath to come through His protection, whose guidance they have already despised, they may judge from past occurrences.

All the wretched reasonings of the profligate in excuse for his offences might have been urged by our first parents; their sin, they might have said, would hurt nobody but themselves: and the Devil his self had suggested to them, that there was no great danger in venturing to indulge their appetites; still the threatened sentence overtook them, and the loss of Paradise and immortality immediately followed that of innocence.

cence. And whose personal experience contradicts this lesson? Reason from what comes daily before you. Will your bodies continue in health without care? If ye conceive that without your making use of the powers He has given you, your Creatour will preserve you from disorders, have ye not hourly proofs of the contrary? How many are now lamenting their own folly in not more carefully attending to the admonitions they received in their younger days, not to lay up for themselves pain and sickness in their old age! And how vain do all their lamentations prove to assuage their sufferings? Apply this reasoning to the case of your souls: perpetually are ye reproved, rebuked, exhorted and called upon a thousand ways, not to do those things in this state, which will bring misery on you in the next; and if ye continue deaf to all the motives (so much more weighty than that of avoiding bodily and temporary sufferings) which are urged to persuade you to refrain from what will prove your condemnation hereafter, will not the permitting you to suffer the evils with which ye were threatened, be a dispensation of the same justice, which leaves the careless in regard to the health of their bodies, to undergo the consequences of their own folly? Or who can deliver you from these sad consequences but He who is Lord, as of this, so of the world to come? And is not this He, whose service, those who follow fleshly lusts, have neglected, whose commandments they have trampled under foot, and whose promises and threatenings they have equally despised?

This particular of our being, by right of creation, servants of God, and our having been again made so by the being purchased with the blood of Christ, seems to be strangely forgotten by many who profess themselves Christians: for, surely, they cannot be ignorant, that it is expected in a servant that he be found faithful. Yet what is his fidelity, who, instead of honestly exerting his abilities, and employing his time in his master's service, wastes both in riotous

riotous living? What is theirs who never think but accidentally of their connection with their Lord, and render Him only the forms of homage? Who, instead of seriously applying their minds to consider what work He hath appointed for them, or how they may most acceptably perform His charge, do, by spending their days between idleness and diversion, prove that they are lovers of pleasure more than lovers of God? When men consider only their temporal evils which the pursuit of their pleasures may bring on them, and indulge themselves as far as they can without incurring these, they plainly manifest a total disregard to the divine censure and approbation: and thus, by bringing them into the condemnation of those who love not God, and obey not the Gospel of Christ, do their lusts war against their souls.

The multitude of victims to the lust of the flesh, and the lust of the eyes, and the pride of life, warrants a presumption, that men are easily drawn aside by these enemies of their salvation, and thus manifests the necessity of exerting all the powers of self-restraint which we possess: as well on account of the encroaching nature of vice, as of the proofs hereby afforded of the frequent execution of the divine menace, that from him who uses it not, shall be taken away even the little grace he has. Is it not, from this desertion and deprivation of the divine illumination and assistance, that we see such instances of abandoned vice? Surely it is through this that so many are deaf to every admonition, dead to all shame of their profligacy; and though they feel the divine judgements beginning to fall on them, in the disgrace, the diseases, the distresses they undergo, proceed with seeming fearlessness to draw down final condemnation on themselves. Surely it is through the gradual diminution of the true light in the breasts of the wicked as their provocations encrease, that we see such encreasing difference between one who continues in innocence, and another who embarks in sin. Compare two females who have taken these

On Purity.

SERM.
I.

these different courses. I do not mean ye should single the instance of vice from the outcasts of society, common prostitutes: there are, alas! sufficient instances without descending to them: and ye will see in the one such an acquired blindness to the evils that hang over her, such insensibility of the criminality of having yielded to fleshly lusts, such a loss of that delicacy and decency of sentiment which remain unimpaired in the other, as will suffer you no longer to doubt, whether in this sense too fleshly lusts do not war against the soul. Or, lastly, compare two persons of these opposite characters in their last scene in this life; I mean their death beds: and examine whether there be no difference in their hopes and in their qualifications for crowns of everlasting life and glory in another state. Consider which has passed as a pilgrim through this world, and appears going to receive from that Lord for whose sake he suffered affliction and reproach, the reward of a faithful servant, that of admission into the joy of his Master; and which has no-

thing

thing but despair remaining: and see the soul of one rising triumphant as the departure from the body approaches; and that of the other already dead in trespasses and sin, expecting nothing but everlasting death from his past submission to fleshly lusts. And as ye would prefer the former of these situations, endeavour to preserve, or gain purity of heart. Every breach in which, ye have seen, rapidly encreases, admitting a train of evil desires, which, spite of the ignorance or sophistry of those who, according to the hardness of their hearts, heap up for themselves indignation against the day of the just judgement of God, do really war against the soul: assured, that although Heaven and earth pass away, the words of Christ shall not pass away, but this declaration of His apostle stand fast for ever, " Without holiness no man shall see the Lord!"

SERMON II.

ON THEFT AND FRAUD.

EPHES. IV. 28.

Let him that ſtole ſteal no more: but rather let him labour, working with his hands the thing which is good, that he may have to give to him that needeth.

IF we may judge of the general ſtate of morals in the ancient Heathen world, by the nefarious crimes countenanced and practiſed by thoſe who have ever been eſteemed the wiſeſt and beſt among their philoſophers, moſt wretched muſt it have been, indeed, at the time when the diſciples of Chriſt went forth, and preached among the nations the neceſſity of repentance unto life.

There existed, it is true, laws in the several communities for the security of the persons and property of men: but when the grossest impurities were encouraged by the pretended examples of their feigned gods, and the actual practice of their most esteemed teachers, the licentiousness of the lower ranks in the gratification of their passions, must have been such as to have placed multitudes of them in perpetual need of those supplies which sober labour alone can give; and we know, from what we at present see in the world, that those who are abandoned to sensual pleasures, are often not very nice as to the means by which they provide themselves money for their extravagance. The suggestion thrown out in the text, therefore, that before their embracing christianity, the crime of theft was among the Gentile converts neither uncommon, nor deemed so heinous as in truth it is, is accounted for by circumstances that must in all probability have existed, and also have called for the precept that contains it, " Let him that stole steal no more."

And,

And, I would I could add, that the necessity of reminding Christians that there is such a commandment ceased with that generation! But, alas! such on the one hand is the want of a just notion of the sacredness of property, and on the other the hypocrisy of men, in calling Christ Lord and Master, while they pay little or no regard to His words, that even this commandment is transgressed by multitudes among us: and it is requisite to represent to them, both the guilt of theft, and that various practices which they are accustomed to disguise with a better name, do in truth partake of it. This then I shall endeavour to do before you in the following discourse, adding to the observations necessary for this purpose, some on the means of avoiding all temptation to dishonesty, and of enabling ourselves to be useful instead of mischievous members of society, recommended by the apostle in the text, " But rather let him labour, working with his hands the thing which is good, that he may have to give to him that needeth."

Now

SERM. II.

Now theft itself confisting in taking away the property of others against the will of the owners, fully to discover the guilt of it, we must consider the sacredness of property; which arises from its being derived originally from the gift of God. For He having made all things is the first owner, and supreme Lord of whatever existeth; and having distributed among His creatures various gifts, blessings, and possessions, whoever seizeth or withholdeth any of these from one to whom they belong, without the authority of the first Giver, or the consent of the party itself, to which the Creatour has, in some cases, given full and absolute dominion over what it possesses, rises in opposition to the dispensations of God, and frustrates, as far as in him lies, His ordinances. While to confirm and secure this dispensation, the Lord having also added His express prohibition, "Thou shalt not steal!" the crime of the thief is two-fold; first, that of disturbing the order which God hath established in the world;

world; and, secondly, that of directly opposing His positive commandment.

Consider the subject under this view of it, and ye will easily discover the futility of all the excuses made for this transgression; as well as the prophaneness of those babblings of the weak and the wicked, who deny the unequal distribution of property in the world to be the dispensation of it's divine Governour, and thus prepare the means of justifying a new partition of it, whenever the needy have power to seize the possessions of the rich.

Still, however, the advocates for open robbery and positive theft are but few in comparison with those who are found ready to defend and to practise, what comes little behind them in criminality: the various frauds I mean practised by men in their dealings with each other. When a man, by a false account of an article of trade, obtains from another a greater sum for it than he is conscious it is worth, Is not this

taking

taking from him by stealth that with which he did not mean to part, and for which he is paid no equivalent? And is not the same in reality a theft? I know that the customs of trade, and other arguments, specious perhaps in the eyes of those who wish them to be true, are urged in justification of the advantages thus taken; But if by a false promise, or a feigned tale, a man be defrauded of money or goods, the offender is acknowledged by all to be a rogue, and to merit the penalty of the laws; and wherein do the cases differ? Does the tradesman spare assurances of the value of his goods, or is he without stories in their praise? Of just so much then as he thus gains beyond their just value he defrauds the buyer; and is guilty of robbery, aggravated by the ingratitude and treachery he returns for the confidence with which his representation is accepted.

In the numberless cases in which advantage is taken of the ignorance of the young or inexperienced to overreach them, and where

where the unsuspicious minds of the credulous are imposed on, (however some of these modes of obtaining money may be countenanced by the example of many of those who call themselves the fashionable world) the same charge of a breach of the eighth commandment will justly lie. For when a man has his property taken from him by means to which he not only has not, and would not have consented, but which he has not even suspected, Is it not stolen from him?

What I have said of the criminality of obtaining an higher price for articles of trade than they are really worth, is so manifestly applicable to selling them deficient in due weight or measure, that it may appear unnecessary to notice this offence separately, as partaking in the guilt of theft. But such is the blindness of men to their own faults, that one who having been imposed on in the purchase of a piece of fine linen, complains of the iniquity of the merchant of whom he bought it, will return

turn to his own house, and there, without remorse, retail wine and strong liquors in measures manufactured on purpose to defraud. Hence it becomes requisite to state, that the portion which is thus holden back from the purchaser, who pays for full measure, is in fact stolen from him, and however common may be offences of this kind, no one guilty of them has yet profited by the lesson of the apostle, and learned to labour, working the thing which is good.

Neither let it be imagined, that the small value of what is thus unfairly taken from each individual, exculpates the offender. For this plea, however commonly used in excuse of those petty thefts, success in which encourages the guilty to proceed to greater, until seized by the hand of justice, and the frequency of which perpetually disturbs the security, and interrupts the comfort of society, is in itself highly absurd: since a man has the same exclusive right to every part of his property, as he hath to the whole; and whether you take a

sum

sum from his treasury, a bottle from his cellar, or a stake from his hedge, you equally deprive him of somewhat that is his own, and thereby become a thief and a robber. And if you are in his service, if you fill any domestick office under him, this your situation, instead of lessening, encreases your crime; and by pilfering from your master, you add treason to your theft. True it is, that to deprive a man of much that belongs to him, is a more cruel deed, a more atrocious crime, but were it less than the value of a single mite, he is a robber who takes it, because it is not the value of the thing taken, but merely the depriving him of what is his own that constitutes the offence. Otherwise, miserable indeed would be the case of the poor, since their small pittance would lie open to every plunderer, and the little value of it tend only to justify the invasion.

Neither, manifestly therefore, can the imagined or real wealth of the person robbed excuse the theft. But how then shall

shall the circumstance of any thing taken belonging to a nation in general, or any less society, render blameless the person who has surreptitiously obtained it? Yet the multitudes of frauds that have been perpetrated, the enormous plunder which has been made with this only plea to distinguish them from theft, almost exceeds the bounds of common calculation. The connections and the rank, as well as the craft of those who are guilty in this respect, oft-times stand between them and justice, but whatever be their station, their criminality may be encreased, but cannot be diminished by it, their true characters are still those of some of the vilest of mankind, and the epithets that justly belong to them are still the same: they are in truth not elevated, but concealed by honours; not dignified, but disguised by titles.

Difficult, indeed, would be the task of enumerating all the practices by which, on the one hand, the community is defrauded, or on the other, individuals are imposed on, while

while the offenders would conceal even from themselves, if they could, the iniquities they commit, by applying to them the gentle names of perquisites of office, customs of trade, and the like. Suffice it to add to what has already been said on this point, let every man so prove his own work, that he may have praise not of men, but of the Lord. And let us now turn our thoughts from this disgusting view of human wickedness to that method which the apostle recommends as a remedy against all real temptation to invade the property of others: " Let him labour, working with his hands the thing which is good."

The most powerful plea that a thief can urge for mercy is, that he was impelled by want to commit the depredation: this plea, therefore, St. Paul has completely obviated, by admonishing us of the duty of that, which, if honestly followed, will keep a man above want; and a little observation will convince you, that the fate of those who become victims to publick justice for this

this crime, may generally be traced to the neglect of sober labour. The sentence originally pronounced on man, that in the sweat of his face he should eat bread, still lies so on the race, that the greater part of the world feel their wants encrease as they cease from working. "I went by the field of the slothful, says the wise man, and by the vineyard of the man void of understanding; and lo, it was grown over with thorns, and nettles had covered the face thereof, and the stone wall thereof was broken down; then I saw, and considered it well: I looked upon it, and received instruction. Yet a little sleep, a little slumber, a little folding of the hands to sleep. So shall thy poverty come as one that travelleth; and thy want as an armed man." As it was in his days so it is in our own. The habitation of the slothful may still be distinguished by its state. Has he a garden, it is an uncultivated desert, the hedge torn up, the ground overrun with weeds; in his house, poverty stares through the broken lattice; his children, ignorant of all but their

their father's example, wander idle in the streets, or roam about the fields, pilfering from their more opulent neighbours what may preserve them from that cold and hunger, againſt which his labour ſhould have defended them: his perſon you may know by the liſtleſs gait, and tattered garment; his goods go piece-meal to be pledged; and ſhould charity ſend him a dinner for his family, he has neither veſſels or fuel to dreſs it. Now when to relieve himſelf from ſuch preſſing neceſſities, the wretch proceeds to lay his hands on his neighbour's property, Is it not his own idleneſs that has created the temptation? and would not labour have kept it both from his door and from his heart?

I ſay from his heart, becauſe thoſe who are properly employed, have not time to think of evil; and becauſe through want of being ſo it is, that many of higher rank are reduced to that point of neceſſity which forces them on unwarrantable means of encreasing their substance. For although a man be not compelled to seek his daily bread by manual labour, is there nothing in which he can employ himself either for his own improvement, or the benefit of society? Yet when useful pursuits are not embraced, to prevent the weight of time, and obviate that tediousness which attends total idleness, a succession of diversions, or a round of company, is sought after, and the great expences attending these, soon impoverish even the wealthy; and reduce them to straights, to deliver themselves from which, those in whom nothing should be seen but what is generous and great, who should be the nerves of the country, connecting the most distant parts with the head, desert their natural situations, their family seats, and conceal themselves in an hired apartment, from the notice to which their rank entitles them, or part with their independence for the sake of profit; if not submit to be guilty of practices which lower them to the level of a swindler.

In truth, whether he be found, among the high or the low, the rich or the poor, an idle man is the peſt of ſociety : and great would be benefits reſulting to mankind, if the rulers of this world would execute the apoſtolic recommendation, " That if a man would not work, neither ſhould he eat." For the encouragement given to idleneſs is not the only evil ariſing from the neglect of this, but what others ſuffer from the want into which the indolent fall, ſhould alſo be taken into conſideration. How many families are reduced to miſery and the extremity of want through the idleneſs of the heads of them ! How many men come in their old age to be ſupported by the charity of their pariſhes, who, had they laboured in their youth as they were able, would not have needed the aſſiſtance of others in their declining years ! And is it honeſt, even in the common ſenſe of the word, for a man to waſte his time and ſtrength when he is conſcious the doing ſo will render him a burthen to others ? Yet is there not reaſon to fear, that many in this country either refuse to labour, or idly spend what they do earn, in their youth, with this very view? that is, from the knowledge that their parishes are obliged to support them, when they are impotent, if they have nothing to maintain themselves? And is not this shamefully abusing the charity of the nation? Or can the bread thus unnecessarily taken from others, some of whom have scarcely sufficient to feed their own families, be said to be well acquired? Let, then, those who are yet in the prime, or the vigour of life, timely consider, what disgrace they will lay up for themselves, nay, to what censure they will justly be exposed, if they, neglecting to employ the powers they now have, are, through this, hereafter reduced to throw themselves on their neighbours for support.

I do not mean by what I have now said to recommend any thing in the least inconsistent with our blessed Lord's commandment, " Lay not up for yourselves treasures on earth," God forbid that any thing I suggest

suggest should be interpreted as advice to omit the least opportunity of doing good for the sake of saving for the morrow which may never come, in contradiction to the doctrine of our divine Master. We know that the Lord will deliver him in the time of trouble who provideth for the sick and needy; and the holy psalmist testifies, that in all his experience, he never saw the righteous forsaken, or his seed begging their bread. And to this security of the divine protection the apostle seems to allude, when in the text he recommends working, not to lay up in store what may not be wanted for our own immediate support, but that we may have wherewithal to give to him that needeth. And although it may, at first sight, appear scarcely necessary to recommend to those who are so well disposed as to be inclined to impart of their earnings to others, that those earnings should be honestly acquired, yet recollection of the inconsistent characters sometimes met with, will convince us, that there are who want

SERM. II.

to be reminded, that if they run in debt with one perſon, that they may give to another, they are, in fact, charitable with other people's money, and are giving to him that needeth that which is by no mean well obtained. Nay, there are even thoſe who imagine that the end will juſtify the means; and that if it be to ſupport the helpleſs, or relieve the poor, they are not to be condemned for the methods by which their money was gained. A doctrine ſubverſive of every principle of righteouſneſs, and which our apoſtle has, in another place, expreſsly condemned. To a world, then, in which ſuch maxims are but too prevalent, the caution to labour only at that which is good was highly neceſſary: and the numbers of thoſe who ſupport themſelves by miniſtering to the vices of others, ſhould be reminded, that they are gaining only to their own deſtruction. For when ſuch come to offer their ſacrifice to their Lord, however coſtly it may be, What is it but the price of guilt?

When

When a man, touched with remorse for iniquitous practices of which he has been guilty, after relinquishing them entirely, sincerely wishes to repair, as much in him lies, the wrong he has done; but through the changes wrought by death, or otherwise around him, can find no one to whom he should make restitution, and therefore distributes the produce of his unjust dealings in charity as a testimony of the reality of his wish to restore them; one would hope the offering of an heart thus sincerely penitent would not be rejected as abominable; but in any case less strong than this, the offerer of unfair gains may well stand in fear of receiving an answer like that of the Lord by His prophet Isaiah, " I hate robbery for burnt-offering." For however those who continue in sin may be ready to give, glad to distribute, it is still the sacrifice of the wicked which they offer, and that is an abomination to the Lord: And how much more if it be given with a wicked heart! As it is, when men imagine they can thus cover their sins, bribing Heaven,

Heaven, as it were, for pardon. Or, when their sins have left them, not they their sins, or, when they have continued in the gains of righteousness, until they think they have secured enough, to imagine that that God will accept what they chuse to set apart for an offering, is it not in the words of holy writ to think, that He is even such an one as theirselves? The very worst generation of the Jews scrupled to put the price of blood into the treasury of the temple, but among us the price of a soul corrupted to its everlasting destruction, is by some thought an offering that can be accepted. How ignorant, how brutish must those be, who entertain such imaginations! He who would become the servant of the God of purity, must be pure his self, " Because it is written, Be ye holy; for I am holy." And the only hope the thief, the extortioner, the unfair dealer in any way, and every one who has worked at that which is not good, has of attaining to repentance unto life is, to give again that which they have robbed, to wash their hands in innocency, and cleanfe their hearts from iniquity, and fo go to the altar, receive the cup of falvation, and call upon the name of the Lord.

SERMON III.

ON THE GOVERNMENT OF THE TONGUE.

St. Matt. xii. 36.

But I say unto you, that every idle word that men speak, they shall give account thereof in the day of judgment: for by thy words thou shalt be justified, and by thy words thou shalt be condemned.

THESE words stand at the close of some observations made by our Lord on offences of the tongue; and the last clause of them, " for by thy words thou shalt be justified, and by thy words thou shalt be condemned," seem to refer to His preceding declaration, that, " Out of the abundance of the heart the mouth speaketh."

Since

SERM. III.

Since the criminality of the words manifestly proceeds from the corruption of the heart by which they are suggested; and as long as the language of the mouth continues to be bad, so long it is plain, some foulness remaineth in the heart. And this observation may well serve as an answer to those who would ask, why it is declared, that our words shall clear or condemn us, whereas, in other parts of Scripture we are told, that men shall be judged according to their works; and there is oftimes a considerable difference between words and actual deeds? For the words, whatever they be, prove the real state of the mind; since, if they be sincere, they certainly do so; and if they be not sincere, they at once prove its falsehood. It is not, therefore, only by the mischief which they do to our neighbours, that our tongues may bring us into judgement, but by the proofs they yield of the wickedness of our hearts; and, under this division, I shall now consider the guilt which we may contract by our words.

The blasphemy of some of the Jews, who ascribed the miracles of our Lord to the power of Beelzebub, gave occasion to the declaration of the text; and although no profane speeches whatever do, as profane, merit the lenient title of idle words, we sometimes meet with men who utter such without seeming sensible of the full import and real criminality of their speeches; and under this view of them such may well be called idle words, as being spoken without the speakers giving themselves the trouble of reflecting on their real signification and tendency, ere they delivered them. But still this very negligence betrays an heart by no mean duely impressed with reverence for that divine Being whose name or dispensations are thus profaned, and, consequently, are not fitly disposed for the kingdom of Heaven. Now among such speeches are to be numbered, all reflections on the providence of God, and the truth of His revelation; the last of which are near akin to the offence censured by our Lord at the time He spake the words before us, since

he

he who doubts the truth of the Gospel, questions the reality of the miracles wrought in its support: all slighting speeches in respect to the importance of religion, all irreverence, quotations and applications of inspired writings, and the placing of any thing relating to the worship of God in a ridiculous light. And while such words betray an heart still defiled with thoughts and principles evil and false, they also affect the hearers of them, who perceiving the utterers of these bold speeches not to be immediately punished for them, thence take courage to follow the sad example: and thus the divine forbearance to the guilty, without which they must perish, does itself add to the number of their crimes; so complex are the chains of sin, so intricate the toils of Satan! But this evil consequence may follow every kind of idle words; to the particular species I am now noticing there is another attached. Of the restraint which religion puts upon their passions men generally wish to get rid, and, consequently, they eagerly catch at every idea that tends

to

to lighten the weight of its authority, or to leſſen the importance of its ſanctions; hence it comes to paſs, that on a mind heſitating between virtue and vice, a random reflection, an inconſiderate word, will make an impreſſion which the ſpeaker neither expected nor intended; and one idle expreſſion determine a ſoul to purſuits leading to everlaſting deſtruction. Let any one who doubts the danger of ſuch an effect, recollect how often his own reſolutions have been determined by the meereſt trifles; how often, when inclination led the ſame way, the leaſt appearance of a reaſon, the leaſt ſhadow of an example, has fixed his choice; and he will then ſee the neceſſity of bridling his tongue, if he would wiſh to keep clear of the guilt of thoſe who cauſe others to offend. If he would wiſh to avoid being covered with the juſteſt confuſion, the beſt grounded terrour on the arrival of that day, when men ſhall give account of every idle word which they have ſpoken.

SERM.
III.
The words of Solomon, " He that hideth hatred with lying lips, and he that uttereth slander, is a fool," by expressing an evil purpose of heart in those who are guilty of these crimes, removes them at once from the class of those mentioned in the text to one of deeper criminality: and thus slander, in whatever shape it appears, under whatever form it endeavours to disguise itself, betrays the existence of malevolence in the heart. Indeed, as it in general springs from envy, the wish to conceal a motive which would so surely discredit every report of the tongue actuated by it, impels the slanderer to assume some false appearance, under which he may deliver, with less danger of detection, the dictates of that passion which rancours in his heart. Sometimes it is surprize at things so unexpected happening that forces the slanderer to break the bonds of silence, and give a detail of what has never happened at all. Sometimes his indignation at vice will not suffer him to be mute, but leads him carefully to delineate enormities that have not been committed:

mitted: and at others, even sympathy itself is pleaded for dwelling upon the feigned errours, losses, or crimes of his neighbours. Nay, do we not sometimes see from that which, with justice and a penetration peculiar to itself, the law of Moses forbad, countenancing a poor man in his cause, occasion is taken, under the fair semblance of disgust at tyranny and oppression, to vent against a superiour malice that has been long brooded in the heart; and his motives are misrepresented, his actions misconstrued, and his character vilified, not for the ostensible reasons then given, but for a grudge of ancient date. And before the Judge, who searcheth the reins and the heart, will such words, think ye, tend to justify or condemn the utterers?

The same question may well be repeated in the case of those who, with malicious pleasure, propagate the evil reports they hear of their acquaintance. It may, perhaps, be true, that they repeat no more than they have heard; what they have so

SERM. III.

heard may likewife be true: But what muft be the heart of him who can fpeak with pleafure of his brother's fhame? Can it be the refidence of love and good-will? Or if his words indicate the abode of fomething very different from thefe therein, when the judgement fhall fit, muft he be juftified or condemned by them? Thefe are points well worthy the ferious confideration of thofe who, while they partake not in the ingenuity, yet fhare in the guilt of the inventors of fcandalous tales, making them their own by the confidence with which they repeat them. Small would be the circle in which the raifer of a mifchievous report could his felf fpread it, it is by the retailers of it that it is carried to the extent to which it reaches; gradually enlarging itfelf like military commands, firft to tens, from tens to hundreds, from hundreds to thoufands, and from thoufands to tens of thoufands; until the original authour of the fcandal is loft in the multitude of his partners in guilt; and the reputation of his victim is generally defamed. Various, indeed,

deed, will be the motives of different individuals in this multitude for the propagation of the tale: while some are evidently impelled by envy, and others manifestly guided by malevolence, some are actuated by the same motives in a less degree, even down to that proportion in which they are almost concealed from themselves; and, in others, the report truely becomes idle words, being uttered merely to fill up the pauses of conversation, without considering the truth or the falsity, the good or evil tendency of what they say. Yet all this while the character of the subject of the scandal is suffering; and after, perhaps, he has seen and acknowledged, and repented of the fault that is so much blazed abroad, censure continues to be heaped on him without remorse; and neither the feelings of his friends and connections, nor the injustice of loading with invective one, who no longer deserves reproach, can stop the wordy torrents of those babblers, who are skilled in little other labour than that of the lips.

SERM. III.

I doubt not but to some persons these, which are daily offences of common conversation, may seem too trifling to deserve notice; but nothing is so among those whose duty it is to strive to go on to perfection; and although trifling indeed are the characters of those idle persons, who wander about from house to house, as tatlers and busy bodies, speaking things which they ought not, yet it may, I conceive, reasonably be doubted, whether they do not hereby nearly as much mischief to society as they are capable of doing; and Can they, think ye, be justified by having done no more than this?

We often hear people reproaching themselves for not having thought before they spake, and lamenting the consequences of their words, when it is too late to prevent them; and the very frequent instances of this would, one might hope, serve as a caution to others against repeating the same folly. But, alas! almost daily are the proofs we receive of the justice of the apostle's obser-

observation, that the tongue setteth on fire the course of nature. For, who can reckon up the secret animosities, the open quarrels, which are occasioned by the mismanagement of it! In fact, to one who attentively considers it, the effect of words upon the human mind seems beyond all estimate: not only the deep offence that a word unadvisedly spoken will give, calls for our attention, but the whimsical temper that men betray in their resentments on this point should impress on us the necessity of circumspection. For, strange as it may appear, experience, I believe, will prove, that it is not at reflections on their moral character that men shew the greatest indignation; a reproach on their judgements, their tastes, and even those for which they are least of all answerable, their persons, is much more eagerly resented: while even those who are not quick in quarrel, feel no less sensibly on such occasions; and the hearts of the gentle and inoffensive are wrung by words, which, if spoken with intention to produce all their effects, would manifest

manifest sad bitterness of spirit; but even when uttered without that, betray a very reprehensible disregard to the peace and comfort of others.

There is a generation who seem to delight in giving vexation where they think they may safely do it; you see them perpetually persecuting, with poignant ridicule and cruel jests, individuals, from whose temper or abilities they imagine themselves secure against the retort they merit. You hear them propagating tales to make such appear ridiculous; and leading them into embarrassment by feigned information. What disposition of soul, then, do the words of these men indicate? Surely not a charitable one in themselves: neither do they tend to promote the growth of it among others. Their most common excuse is, that they were but in sport. But to sport with the sufferings of others is, under the most favourable interpretation, the characteristick of him to whom Solomon applies it, "As a madman who casteth firebrands, arrows,

and

and death, so is he that deceiveth his neighbour, and saith, Am I not in sport?" And the errours into which they lead those whom they make their dupes, may, with great ease, thus give rise to disgust, animosity, and contention. And can we suppose the authours of such evils will be justified by their words?

If not, however, what shall we think of the tale bearer, for those are the natural fruits of his labours; so much so, indeed, that the wise king seemeth to ascribe the continuance of strife exclusively to him; " Where no wood is, there the fire goeth out: so where there is no tale bearer, the strife ceaseth." (Prov. xxvi. 20.) And in another place; " He that covereth a transgression, seeketh love; but he that repeateth a matter, separateth very friends." Nay, the divine lawgiver his self saw sufficient in this practice to require an express prohibition; and we read, in the 16th verse of the 19th chapter of Leviticus, " Thou shalt not go up and down as a tale bearer among thy people,"

people," coupled with, "Neither shalt thou stand against the blood of thy neighbour," and supported by that solemn and sublime clause of authority, "I am the Lord." If we may judge from the multitudes of mistakes of the kind, it is a very difficult thing accurately to represent to another the words or the deeds of a third person: and individuals differ so much not only in their modes of expression, but in their conception, that it seems almost impossible, that a thing given at second hand should not vary in some measure from the original; yet that troublesome generation who tell of such things as pertain not to them, are generally confident that they repeat them as they heard them; and thus are kindled flames of contention that at length alarm the authours of them, and lead them to ask, with all the vacant wonder of the fool, Who would have supposed what they did so innocently would have produced such consequences? For I am far from meaning to insinuate, that all talebearers are guilty of intentional mischief:

be

be it acknowledged, that their words are only idle words, yet since these are forbidden, they are, while uttering them, doing that which is unlawful: and if, by committing this, they occasion evils which they never intended, it highly becomes them to consider, whether for such evils they may not justly be called into judgement.

The same flimsy excuse of meaning no harm, is pleaded by some, who take still greater liberties in speech; and we hear men convicted of falsehood urge, that they did not intend to hurt any one by what they said: but even if they affirm, as others will boldly plead, that their object was to do good thereby, so far from making a sound defence, they are only confessing themselves guilty of what the apostle so strongly reprobates by asserting, that just is the damnation of those who say, Let us do evil that good may come. How much less then, when they break the divine commandment, Lye not one to another,—for the sake of appearing to be endued with wit,

or

or possessed of some excellence which they have not! These are far from idle words being uttered on purpose to deceive; and with the multitude of others that are so, to conceal faults, avoid anger, or gain favour, when brought to accompt in the day of judgement, must tend to condemn those who are guilty of them of lying lips, and a deceitful tongue. Indeed, these last often contain false accusations of others, either directly made, or conveyed in hints not to be misunderstood; or by assuming the merit which in truth belongs to others, rob them of their due recompence, and are really breaches of the ninth commandment.

Neither among mere idle words are to be ranked that foolish talking and jesting, which the apostle says, become not Christians; conversation, I mean, replete with those coarse jests and obscene images in which the profligate and lascivious delight to deal. When men use gross expressions without appearing to be sensible of the indecency of them, What is this but a mark that

that they have deftroyed all fenfe of purity from their minds? and if they are fenfible of what they utter, How foul muft be thofe hearts, from the abundance of which proceedeth an almoft continued ftream of filthinefs? The mifchief perpetrated by men of this character is not limited to the confufion with which loofe difcourfe covers the innocent and modeft: from caufing this, perhaps, they are, in many cafes, careful to refrain; but both their words and example tend to the corruption of the young, to encourage them in vices to which they are already too much inclined, and to enflame their appetites which are already difficult to be controuled: And how fhall thofe words be juftified which caufe one of the little ones that believe in Chrift to offend?

The worft of thofe which can juftly be termed idle words, are fuch as while we doubt whether we fhould utter them or not, becaufe the nature of them feems undecided, we yet deliver in the mere wantonnefs of fpeech. When, therefore, we are fo little fcrupulous scrupulous of running the hazard of a crime, if we actually commit one, Can we wonder that we shall be called into judgement for it? "In a multitude of words," saith Solomon, "there wanteth not sin." And if we consider the vanity of the opinions, the badness of the maxims, and the falsity of the assertions, which great talkers deliver, we shall see sufficient reason to assent to the justice of the observation; and particularly so in regard to that profusion of asseveration which they use, protesting by every thing that should be sacred, the truth of the most unimportant matters. In fine, crimes of the same kind, although not of the same degree, and mischief of the same sort, although not of the same extent, are committed by the idle babbler, as by the intentional offender; and since we are warned against the evils of this practice, we are, in the purest justice, answerable for whatever we may occasion by neglecting the admonition. Let it therefore sink deep into your minds, that "death and life are in the power of the tongue: and they that love

love it shall eat the fruit thereof." That "he that can rule his tongue shall live without strife; and he that hateth babbling shall have less evil. Rehearse not unto another that which is told unto thee, and thou shalt fare never the worse. Whether it be to a friend or a foe, talk not of other men's lives; and if thou canst without offence, reveal them not. If thou hast heard a word, let it die with thee; and be bold, it will not burst thee." Remember, that trifling in sense as may be the multitude of words that are spoken, they are far from trifling in their consequences; since by them it will be determined, whether we are worthy to be admitted to an inheritance in that everlasting kingdom of purity, peace, and righteousness, which is ready to be revealed: and as ye would not risque your final lot on the babblings of an heedless tongue, let the solemn words of Him from whose mouth your last sentence must proceed, serve you as a perpetual admonition to circumspection and restraint. "But I say

say unto you, that every idle word that men speak, they shall give account thereof in the day of judgement: for by thy words thou shalt be justified, and by thy words thou shalt be condemned."

SERMON IV.

ON COVETOUSNESS.

EXOD. XX. 17.

Thou shalt not covet thy neighbour's house; thou shalt not covet thy neighbour's wife, nor his man-servant, nor his maid-servant, nor his ox, nor his ass, nor any thing that is thy neighbour's.

IN the sad list of those vices which St. Paul hath forewarned Christians should, with unbridled licence, overrun the world in the perilous times of the last days, selfishness and covetousness hold the first places; " This know also," says that most vigilant minister of Christ, " that in the last days perilous times shall come. For men shall be lovers of their own selves, covetous, boasters, proud, blasphemers," and so on. It is true, an ingenious disputant might here demand, " In what age have not men been selfish and covetous?" But the words of the apostle plainly point to a peculiar prevalence of these vices, and that in a degree which should affect the general safety of believers; " Perilous times shall come."—Days of difficulty and hazard.

The true and important question therefore is, Have we ourselves lived to see times of this description? And as this is the proper question to be asked, so is it one that is easily resolved. For can we not of our own knowledge testify, that licentiousness is risen to such a height, and apostacy from the faith become so common, as to multiply the temptations, and encrease the difficulties of those who would yet continue in the doctrine of the Gospel? Have we not seen a very numerous nation publickly renounce christianity, and put many who would not join in the general impiety, to death,

death, for their adherence to religion? And have not the two vices which stand at the head of the catalogue left us by St. Paul, had a very great influence in producing this state of things? Consider what first opened a door to the confusion, the excesses, and the miseries, that have overrun that wretched land? What first took off all the salutary restraints that regular government, a sense of religion, and respect for authority imposed on the passions of its inhabitants? Was it not the desire of some individuals to supplant others in the dignities and the emoluments they possessed? And what was this but covetousness? What gave rise to the doctrine of equality, but the desire of those who had little, to partake of what belonged to those who had much? Or what has caused the same doctrine to find so many favourers in our own country, but an evil eye at the superiour power, or more ample possessions, of those who are greater or richer than theirselves? The leaders of the guilty, it is true, hold out other pretences for their conduct: but this they do, because

because the publication of a motive so foul, would doubtlessly prevent their success; not because they have any repugnance to own their disregard of the precepts of religion, since these they are insane enough most openly to deride. To this more exceeding sinful point of sin, many of their followers, we may hope, would not willingly accompany them; but being deceived by reasonings cunningly devised to mislead, they have, ere they were aware, been seduced to act directly contrary to His laws, whom they still own for their God and their Saviour; although they would be unfeignedly shocked at thinking they had presumptuously trampled on His commandments. For such then, and for others, who, without timely admonition, might suffer themselves to be brought into the same situation, lest any such teachers should come among you, I shall now investigate the divine precept contained in the text, and shew how totally inconsistent with it are those levelling doctrines which such various means are used

used to instil into the hearts of the people of this land.

This commandment, ye know, stands the last of the ten; and it seems to have been there placed, because obedience to it is a sure mean of securing a compleat compliance with those that precede it: since he who does not covet his neighbour's wife, or his neighbour's goods, will scarcely proceed to adultery or theft. It appears here, likewise, as the seal of Heaven to the sacredness of property; and gives the sanction of God Almighty to that exclusive right which every man has over all that is his own; whether it be much, or whether it be little. On which account it seems to be but a natural step in the progress of vice, for those who have once embraced principles destructive of this right, to proceed to deny the authority of God Himself, against whom they have already rebelled in fact. And in what must this course begun in covetousness end but in misery? Or if all men were to give way to this vice, (and if one may practice it without guilt, surely all may) Would not the earth exhibit only a scene of rapine, murder, and inexpressible distress?

It is under the pretence of friendship to the lower ranks of men, that the propagators of the doctrine of equality endeavour to forward their system. But mark the fruits of this friendship in the natural order in which they arise; or, in other words, observe the curse which, by His original constitution of things, God hath affixed to the breach of this His statute, " Thou shalt not covet." When a man begins to imagine that he should be happier if he had some possession of his neighbour's, he no longer enjoys the peace of mind that flows from content. Incapable of deriving satisfaction from what he has, because his wishes are anxiously fixed upon something yet unobtained, he consumes, in all the solicitude of desire, that time which, but for improper inclinations being raised in his mind, might have been passed in comfort:

so

so falsely do those who excite such wishes in our breasts stile themselves our *friends!* But if, to free himself from the disquietude of desire, he proceed to obtain by fraud or force the possession which he covets, of a neighbour he makes an enemy, and becomes exposed to all the penalties which may justly be exacted from the thief or the robber.

Similar to what it thus produces in the case of an individual, are the effects of covetousness when it is excited in a multitude: experiencing separately the same uneasiness, they become collectively restless; and by communicating their complaints, they mutually inflame each other's minds, till bursting the chains of fear, as they have before broken the bands of conscience, they assert, by brute force, the claims which justice would not support: the rightful possessors of the goods desired, are thus reduced to violent means of self-defence; and all the horrours of civil war, of natural consequence, ensue.

This,

SERM. IV.

This, it *must* be acknowledged, would be the cafe, where the party that wifhes to gain, and that which is unwilling to lofe, are nearly equal in number or in power; but if the friends of the levelling fyftem are willing to fuppofe a courfe of events more favourable to their fchemes, and that the multitude of their affociates would at once reprefs all oppofition, and thus put them in poffeffion of that fhare of good things which they wifh to have, let us examine what would then be the confequence.

Would not the acquifition of what was at firft demanded only lead to further requifition? Would not the gratification of fome defires caufe others likewife to arife? This a little obfervation will demonftrate to you is the common progrefs of human appetite. If it were not, we fhould be able to point out fome degree of wealth and power at which, when men arrive, they are in general content to ftop. But whoever heard of that point? Look at thofe around

around you, whofe fituation in life has been improved; are they not reaching at fomething further? Or enquire of your own heart; Are ye at all more fatisfied with your ftate now, than ye were years ago; when ye imagined, that ye could by this time have obtained fomething, that would have fecured your contentment? Confider any above you whofe places ye would be moft defirous of occupying: ye will find that they too have their troubles; and, if thofe who from their infancy were prepared for fuch fituations, meet with cares in them, Would not ye who are unufed to them find ftill more?

Behold, then, the folly of that covetoufnefs with which defigning men ftrive to enflame the minds of the poorer part of the community. Being, from its origin, a tranfgreffion of the laws of God, like every breach of thofe perfect ordinances, it neceffarily tends to the mifery of the tranfgreffors; and even if, without noticing the enormous crimes which muft be committed, and

and the almost insuperable difficulties that must be overcome, ere such a thing could be accomplished, we for a moment suppose that perfect state of equality introduced into society, which none but the most ignorant of men, or those of disordered intellects, can imagine feasible; the taking away all inequality of possession would not extinguish covetousness; because a man's neighbour not having more than he, will not prevent him from the wishing to have more than his neighbour: and though there would be none in the race of life to overtake, there would still be all to leave behind; which would be an equally strong spur to the passions, of either avaricious or ambitious men.

It being, therefore, contrary to the nature of the human passions to be cured by indulgence, and especially so to that of one which being not bodily but mental, is not weakened or extinguished by the debility or age of the body; and this, by the just appointment of Heaven, leading, while it does

does continue to prevail in our breasts, only to misery: What have we to do but to repress, and, if possible, to root all covetous desires out of our hearts? To induce you to set about a work so salutary, so productive of peace, so necessary to your happiness, to the statement I have already made of the folly of indulging this passion, let me now add that of its guilt, as comprehending injustice to man, and impiety towards God.

Strange as it may appear, that in this land where so much pains are taken to instruct the poorest of the people in the great principles of morality, there should be any who can enter upon a course of conduct replete with iniquity, and yet not be sensible of the injustice of it; yet, I believe, it is true, that many have listened with pleasure to proposals for levelling the distinctions, and making a new distribution of the possessions of the country, without being at all stricken with the nefarious wickedness of the scheme proposed. Engrossed with the thought of gaining by the change, and of partaking

partaking in what their superiours now enjoy, they never considered whether, if they were in the situation of those who were to be plundered, they should be willing to have their property in like manner taken from them?

Yet the very lowest rule of justice is, not to do that unto another, which we would not he should do unto us. Had this been observed, What numerous malignant aspersions cast upon the higher orders of society, how many misrepresentations made to render them hateful in the eyes of the inferiour classes, would have been buried in silence; because the utterers would not like such calumnies to be spoken of themselves! Had this been observed, how early would have been rejected every idea of conspiracy, to strip of their legal rights, and attack in their lawful possessions, those who were raised by their rank or property above the commonalty of the land! For are the boldest leaders, the most obstinate supporters of such conspiracy, inclined to have any rights

rights theirselves claim, trampled on, or any property they may possess, taken from them? If not, the application of this maxim of justice shews at once the hideous deformity of their conduct. While comparing that conduct with the prohibition of the text, will no less quickly shew how exposed it is to the divine vengeance. For thus saith the Lord, " Thou shalt not covet (not only thy neighbour's house, wife, servants, or cattle, but) any thing that is thy neighbour's."

Now, is it possible, any man could entertain a thought of joining with others to take a portion of his neighbour's property, and divide it among themselves, without transgressing this commandment? For observe, it is the very wish that is forbidden; nor is the prohibition restrained to the particulars enumerated, but is extended universally to every thing that is thy neighbour's: and we cannot envy a man for his wealth, his privileges, or his place, without breaking this precept of the Governour of of the univerfe. That much uneafinefs, and many fufferings, naturally attend the tranfgreffion of it, I have before fhewn in ftating, that a man no fooner begins to defire any part of his neighbour's property, than he forfeits the tranquillity of his own mind; that it opens the way to contention, and, in its progrefs, neceffarily produces hoftilities. I muft now call your minds to the manifeft judgements which God hath been pleafed to inflict on fome who have more efpecially difregarded this commandment.

The firft ftep towards coveting what is our neighbour's, is becoming difcontented with what ourfelves poffefs; a ftate of temper which generally breaks forth into murmuring againft the difpenfations of Providence; and which we are, by an apoftle, cautioned to avoid, by the example of the Ifraelites, who, in the defert, perifhed through the fame ungrateful behaviour: "Neither murmur ye as fome of them alfo murmured, and were deftroyed of the deftroyer."
From

From being discontented with our own goods to envying those of others, is an easy transition; and then is our breach of the commandment perfect. The tremendous manifestation of the divine wrath on both these crimes, is thus described by the psalmist: " They lusted exceedingly in the wilderness, and tempted God in the desert, and He gave them their request, but sent leanness into their soul. They envied Moses also in the camp, and Aaron the saint of the Lord. The earth opened and swallowed up Dathan, and covered the congregation of Abiram; and a fire was kindled in their company; and the flame burnt up the wicked." And what shall I say more? For the time would fail me to tell of those who, in the pursuits of ambition and avarice, both forbidden by the tenth commandment, have been made to eat the fruit of their own doings, and, like the discontented Israelites, perished while the meat was yet in their mouths.

SERM. IV.

There is, however, an inftance fo near our own doors, fo pregnant with inftruction peculiarly adapted to ourfelves, that it would fcarcely be lefs than leaving unnoticed a marked leffon of the Almighty, to clofe this difcourfe without mentioning it. That nation which, awhile ago, was holden up to the inhabitants of this land as fetting a bright example of wifdom, and as having difcovered a method of raifing themfelves to an unprecedented height of glory and happinefs, and as preparing the way for the reign of peace and felicity over all the earth: that nation, I fay, having firft feized the wealth of all the opulent among themfelves, then broken into the adjoining countries, and plundered the inhabitants of them, are now ftarving in the midft of their neighbour's poffeffions. They, indeed, not only broke the divine commandments, but, with the moft daring impiety, blafphemed and denied God and His Chrift, wherefore the Lord feems to have taken their punifhment more immediately into His own hands, the nations which

which their nefarious conduct raised against them, have met with little success in the war, yet are the people who call themselves victorious, reduced to the lowest state of misery. The sword having passed through their land in its most dreadful shapes, the pike of the conspirator, the dagger of the assassin, and the axe of the executioner, different adventurers have, by turns, gained the command both of the power and purse of the country, until the people, equally fleeced by all, have lost all sensibility through their sufferings, and lie in the lowest state of human degradation; deprived of all the comforts of this life, and incapable of drawing consolation from the hope of another. Let us, then, as witnesses of these just afflictions, give glory to God, and confess the equity of the sentence uttered by His prophet; " Woe be to him that coveteth an evil covetousness to his house, that he may set his nest on high, that he may be delivered from the power of evil. Thou hast consulted shame to thy house, by cutting off many people, and hast sinned against thy

thy soul. For the stone shall cry out of the wall, and the beam out of the timber shall answer it. Woe be to him that buildeth a town with blood, and establisheth a city by iniquity. Behold, Is it not of the Lord of hosts, that the people shall labour in the very fire, and the people shall weary themselves for very vanity?" And let us, if we would not bring down the same calamities on our country, and ourselves, learn from this most impressive example, that covetousness leads not to riches; that though men should prove too weak to resist the plundered, the Lord He is strong: and if, by attacking the former, ye break the laws of the latter; though following the common course of wickedness, ye, after putting away a good conscience, make shipwreck of faith, and deny God, He cannot deny Himself, but is to day the same, who in times past declared, "Vengeance is mine, I will repay, saith the Lord!" Humble yourselves, therefore, under the mighty hand of God; when suffering, commit your cause unto Him that judgeth righteously; then,

then, when He shall be revealed, taking vengeance on those who knew not Him, and obey not the Gospel of his Son, instead of hiding your faces with terrour from Him Who sitteth on the throne, ye shall rejoice at His appearance, and glory in the God of your salvation!

SERMON V.

ON THE LOVE OF OUR NEIGHBOUR.

Rom. xiii. 8.

Owe no man any thing, but to love one another: for he that loveth another hath fulfilled the law.

THE delivery of this general rule is preceded by the mention of several particulars, in which the apostle directeth its application: and the turn of expression used in it appears to have been occasioned by the terms he had employed in recommending those particulars: " Render to all their dues: tribute to whom tribute is due, custom to whom custom, fear to whom fear, honour to whom honour. Owe no man any thing but to love one another.'

The strength of language here to be gained by the change of phrase, could not escape so able a master of reasoning as St. Paul; and he has used it in its full extent; suddenly striking to our hearts the lesson that our love of one another is a debt which we should deem never to be compleatly discharged; while, by continuing in the payment of it, we shall fulfil the law which contains our duty towards our neighbour. For to the commandments of the second table only does he seem here to have respect; since he immediately subjoins, "For this thou shalt not commit adultery, thou shalt not kill, thou shalt not steal, thou shalt not bear false witness; and if there be any other commandment, (as there is, honour thy father and thy mother) it is briefly comprehended in this saying, namely, thou shalt love thy neighbour as thyself." Which limitation of the apostle's meaning I would particularly recommend to your attention, as tending to expose, in this case, the reasoning of a generation now but too numerous, who have embraced a very summary

mary method of easing themselves from the burthen of the particular precepts of religion, by persuading themselves, that their whole duty is contained in an ineffective benevolence, sheltered behind their pretensions to which they lie insensible to the calls of truth, justice, and piety. There may be others also to whom, although they be not so far advanced in errour, the setting of the injunction of the text in its proper light may afford an useful admonition.

It is, then, an active principle, by the entertainment of which we are here taught that the law is fulfilled, and whatever is less than that, is not the thing meant to be inculcated: owe no man any thing but love, is, render to all their dues with that readiness, sincerity, and integrity, which the feelings of affection, as well as the sense of justice, dictate: and it is clearly at the so compleat discharge of all the social duties, of every charitable office, that nothing shall remain unpaid, that this precept is directed, in opposition to the backwardness and partiality

tiality which men are apt to betray in the performance of them, and the evil ingenuity they shew in framing systems to elude the force of the commandments: the envious man cannot conceive, how his propagating an evil report, which his malice makes him believe to be true, can be a breach of the ninth commandment; neither can a covetous man imagine, what the advantages he takes, can have to do with the crime forbidden by the eighth; while many, who perhaps think themselves entitled to the character of benevolent, have nothing to urge in support of their claim, but that they do no harm to any body. How different is this from the principle the text would inculcate, that our debt of kindness is never discharged, but that as long as there are any good offices we can do, so long do we continue to owe them! It is true, the apostle says, that love is the fulfilling of the law, because it worketh no ill; but, surely, he never meant to restrain its operation to this, when he has his self given so many precepts that extend beyond it;

it; and when his divine Master had formally delivered rules of action in addition to those of the law, and expressly called this very commandment in the extent in which He gave it, a new one. " A new commandment give I unto you, that ye love one other; as I have loved you, that ye also love one another."

Far from this, too, there were in the law of Moses several positive precepts, exemplifying the manner in which the general commandment, " Thou shalt love thy neighbour as thyself," was to be applied to practice: and would Christians occasionally peruse these, they might gather from them useful hints towards complying with the exhortation of St. John, " My little children, let us not love in word, neither in tongue, but in deed, and in truth."

That carelessness in respect to the property of others, which is often manifested among us, and is so incompatible with real regard for the owners of it, will appear highly

highly opprobrious to those who live under an higher dispensation, if compared with the following precept of Moses: "Thou shalt not see thy brother's ox, or his sheep astray, and hide thyself from them: thou shalt in any case bring them again unto thy brother. And if thy brother be not nigh unto thee, then thou shalt bring it into thine own house, and it shall be with thee until thy brother seek after it, and thou shalt restore it to him again. In like manner shall thou do with his ass; and so shalt thou do with his raiment; and with all lost things of thy brother's which he hath lost, and thou hast found, shalt thou do likewise: thou mayest not hide thyself." Deut. xxii. 1—3.

Compare with this direction the readiness with which some, who yet would not be called uncharitable, apply to their own use what they find belonging to others. Compare with it the insensibility with which others will waste, or destroy what is their neighbour's; from the lawless hunter, who demo-

demolishes the fences, and tramples down the crops of the husbandman, to the wasteful domestick, who pleads his master's supposed wealth for needlesly consuming his substance: and ye will then see, that while the law commanded no more than the real practice of the love it had enjoined, the pretended disciples of the Gospel, prove the conformity of their lives with it, by doing deeds of hatred to their neighbours.

Again, it was said to them of old time, "If there be among you a poor man of one of thy brethren within any of thy gates in thy land which the Lord thy God giveth thee, thou shalt not harden thine heart, nor shut thine hand from thy poor brother: but thou shalt open thine hand unto him, and shalt surely lend him sufficient for his need, in that which he wanteth. Beware that there be not a thought in thy wicked heart, saying, The seventh year, the year of release, is at hand; and thine eye be evil against thy poor brother, and thou givest him nought; and he cry unto the Lord against

against thee, and it be sin unto thee. Thou shalt surely give him, and thine heart shall not be grieved when thou givest him: because that for this thing the Lord thy God shall bless thee in all thy works, and in all thou puttest thine hand unto. For the poor shall never cease out of thy land: therefore I command thee, saying, Thou shalt open thine hand wide unto thy brother, to thy poor, and to thy needy, in thy land." Deut. xv. 7—11.

To say that the generous bounty here commanded is seldom practised in our land, would be doing gross injustice to many among us: But is there not yet a remnant whose behaviour calls for the admonition; who imagine that they have satisfied every obligation incumbent on them if they have not taken or withholden the property of others, and have no conception of the debt mentioned in the text, " to love one another?" The pleas which such use for saving their money, that it was through their own imprudence that those who need
their

their affiftance, became poor, that every man has difficulties enough of his own to ftruggle with, and the like, are by no mean allowed in the law. How much farther, then, muft they be from availing aught under the Gofpel, of which the diftinguifhing commandment is, that we love one another as Chrift loved us? For He loved us fo, as to fuffer for us; to love, as He loved, therefore, we muft be ready to put ourfelves to inconvenience, nay, and to fomething more, if that be neceffary, for the relief of a brother; and by this fhall all men know, that we are His difciples.

The laft Mofaical precept I fhall notice runs thus: " Thou fhalt in any wife rebuke thy neighbour, and not fuffer fin upon him." Lev. xix. 17. Affection really warm, overlooks no intereft of the object of its love; and daily are the inftances of anxiety manifefted to fecure to perfons beloved, the favourable regards of thofe whofe patronage may be of ufe to them in the world; the friendfhip of thefe they are advifed vised to cultivate, by all means, against giving any offence to these, are they most earnestly cautioned: or if, through want of such caution, they do forfeit the favour of any who might have assisted them, the persons by whom the caution ought to have been given, are censured, as deficient in that attention which affectionate attachment dictates. Now if the rebuke thus passed be just, surely, in the more important case of offences against God, it becomes an office of charity to reprove, rebuke, exhort; and, in proportion to our belief in the reality of His superintendance, the universality of His providence, the severity of his judgements, and the certainty of His rewards to them who walk in His laws, will naturally be our earnestness to preserve all whom we love from incurring His indignation, or forfeiting His protection. In Christians, therefore, who are taught that the sanctions of the divine commandments are according to the perfection of Him who ordained them, this care will, if our love be real, take place of all others; and were we to act adequately

to

to our profession, our conduct would thus be the practice of the noblest of all principles under the highest improvement.

Neglect of duty, and transgressions of the law, do, in general, manifestly arise from selfishness; the completion of our duty, and the fulfilling of the law, should, therefore, it should seem, spring from the contrary principle; and a ready and sincere discharge of all the social offices, can be secured only by brotherly love being fixed in our breasts. In deeds of kindness, in acts suggested by benevolence, the heart goes before the hand, and the works of this last seldom equal the wishes of the former. Neither are the merits of the objects of our love scrupulously weighed. If they appear to need our assistance, if an opportunity of obliging them offer, much is easily forgotten, much is immediately forgiven; and by the natural operation of this principle, we become merciful, even as our Father which is in Heaven is merciful, shewing kindness, and conferring favours even on the thankless and ungrateful.

Did

SERM. V.

Did such a principle then reign in the breasts of all the human race, what a perfect cessation of all injuries, what an uninterrupted exchange of good offices would it produce! What sobriety of conduct, what abstinence would it cause in life! not only on account of the other effects which the indulgence of ourselves may have on the welfare or comfort of others, but from the effectual recollection which would then take place, that by refraining from the needless expence of time or money, we should be enabled to contribute much more largely to the assistance of our brethren. None would then pine in want, neither would any be found friendless. The hardships flowing from prepossession and prejudice would cease: and the disappointments arising from the varying resolves, and the uncertainty of the attachments of men, would be no more; for universal benevolence must be without partiality, and sincere love without hypocrisy.

On the Love of our Neighbour.

From the perfection of this principle of action, it may juftly be inferred, that if it pleafed the Creatour of the world to reveal a rule of life to mankind, this would be found therein: Yet where is it to be met with as the great law of behaviour, that to which all others are reducible, and by their confonance with which they are perfected, but in the Chriftian Scriptures, or the fayings of thofe who have borrowed from them? And is it to be believed, that a few fifhermen of Galilee could, without fupernatural affiftance, have difcovered and dilated, with the moft judicious accuracy, on a maxim, the comprehenfive fimplicity and excellence of which had efcaped the fagacity and earneft refearches of the wifeft of the Greeks? Or, fince they did teach the world this great rule, Did they not, without controverfy, in thus delivering their Mafter's words, fpeak as never men fpake?

To the congruity of this principle to the unvitiated affections and beft reafonings of the human mind, the bittereft enemies of the Gospel in our days, have borne most ample and unequivocal testimony, by adopting a pretension to it, as the surest mean of making proselytes to their sect. But while universal benevolence and brotherly love are their ostensible motives, and their professed aim is to make men happy, by making them good, by not practising this principle under the relations they already bear to those around them, they both manifest the hypocrisy of their professions, and yield to all, whose eyes the God of this world hath not blinded, that they should not believe, a fearful lesson against leaving the sure instruction of revelation, for fanciful motives of action. When men, instead of trusting the general happiness of the world to the care of its almighty Governour, absurdly and presumptuously extend their aims beyond the contracted sphere to which their own powers can reach, far from preserving the peace of society, and contributing to the benefit of others, by neglecting the humble, though real duties, of the individual, and affecting a character of extensive import-

importance, which belongs not to them, they disturb the tranquillity of the world, and are led to the commission of the most unpardonable aggressions, the most enormous crimes. Thus it is that these pretenders to benevolence have signalized themselves by the grossness of their transgression of every one of those commandments, obedience to which the apostle exhorts us to complete, by loving one another.

The honour due to parents, and the natural affection subsisting between individuals related by blood, they require all, who are sufficiently infatuated to associate with them absolutely to renounce; thus destroying from among them all obedience to the first of the laws relating to our neighbour; the second of these they set at nought, by putting to death, in any secure way, those who present themselves as powerful opponents to their pretendedly great, though, in truth, nefarious and horridly pernicious projects. The prohibition of adultery, it is well known, they have treated as of no autho-

authority. And the uneftimated plunder, the atrocious robberies of the armies under the direction of this fect, whofe object, it has been repeatedly declared, is like that of the fect itfelf, the deftruction of all the kings of the earth, fufficiently prove, that their love is not manifefted by tendernefs for the property of their neighbours. While the bitter calumnies with which they purfue all who attempt to expofe their fophiftry, and put men on their guard againft their impious and deftructive plans, the railing accufations they bring againft all in authority, and the diftruft they endeavour to fow among thofe, who, if united, would be ftrong enough to crufh their machinations, convict them, fpite of all their pretenfions to benevolence, of bearing falfe witnefs. And, laftly, their covetoufnefs has, it fhould feem, been the grand motive for feizing the wealth, the power, and the firft honours of the countries given by the divine juftice into their hands: fo perfectly have they, in their courfe, trampled under foot every law by which the perfons, the property, and the

the rights of men are secured. Whereas, had they in fact rendered, as we are commanded, love to every one, not one of these crimes would have been committed; they might have been harmless, and the world have had no complaint against them.

The apostolick injunction before us is, ye may easily perceive, calculated to prevent every aggression, to repress every crime in the very bud; nor could the force of it, for this purpose, be evaded, but by the introduction of a doctrine which St. Paul has forewarned every Christian to consider as holden by those whose damnation is just, that of doing evil that good may come of it. By this detestable tenet, men either arrogate to themselves the power of securing success to their measures, or profanely assert, that God will bless the wicked in their deeds, and patronize the transgressours of His own laws; when reason, experience, and Scripture, all join in teaching, that He who once presumes to break a commandment of the Lord, not only forfeits all claim to, but really loses, in some degree, the divine assistance; that one transgression leads to another, diminishing our power of resisting temptation, and lessening our abhorrence of evil.

Let it be remembered, therefore, that the commandment we have received, to love one another, is universal: and that not merely as to its objects, but in respect likewise to the particulars in which we should manifest this love; in care of the property, respect to the rights, regard to the reputation, and attention to the feelings of our brethren. When we wilfully assault, or obstinately disregard any of these, we break the royal law, " Thou shalt love thy neighbour as thyself:" and be the excuses we may pretend, what they may, even if we plead, that we were seeking the honour of God, we are guilty of gross hypocrisy, in affecting to seek His honour through the breach of His commandments. Obedience to these is the mean by which perfect wisdom has ordained, that we should contribute to to the general good: and while we mourn with those that mourn, and rejoice with those that do rejoice, we do not fancifully, but really contribute, to the general stock of comfort and happiness, and love not in word only, but in deed, and in truth.

How to make this the great principle of our conduct, we have received both instruction and encouragement from Him in whom alone, of all the sons of man, our heavenly Father could be well pleased. He, far from becoming an aggressor, shewed His love even to His persecutors, by the patience with which He submitted to all the injuries they heaped on Him. When He was reviled, He reviled not again; when He suffered, He threatened not; but pitied us, even when we were His enemies, and underwent miseries that belonged not to Him, that He might relieve us, while we were yet sinners; and thus pitying us in our lowest state of misery, not of body only, but of soul, extended His solicitude for us beyond the present to a future state; and thus

SERM. V.

thus exhibited to the human race a new subject on which to exercise mutual benevolence, the attainment of happiness in another life. Zeal on this point it is, that particularly distinguishes the Christian. Whether in a private station as a parent, a master, or a friend, or in publick as a member of the commonwealth, or a magistrate, if he have any sense of the inheritance to which he is called with his brethren, he will not cease to rebuke, command, exhort, that men live soberly, righteously, and godly, as holding that blessed hope, and looking for the glorious appearance of Him who having died, that we might live for ever, has commanded us to love one another as He loved us; And can we do this if we be thoughtless of the future fate, careless of the salvation of our brethren? Herein, then, let our love be made perfect, that we may have boldness in the day of judgement; because as He was, so are we in this world!

SERMON VI.

ON THE LORD'S SUPPER.

---

1 Cor. xi. 26.

For as often as ye eat this bread, and drink this cup, ye do shew the Lord's death till He come.

WE read in the book of Exodus, that at the institution of the passover, Moses commanded the children of Israel, saying, " And ye shall observe this thing for an ordinance to thee, and to thy sons, for ever. And it shall come to pass when ye be come to the land which the Lord will give you according as He hath promised, that ye shall keep this service. And it shall come to pass when your children shall say unto you, What mean you by this service ?
That

SERM.
VI.
That ye shall say, It is the sacrifice of the Lord's passover, who passed over the houses of the children of Israel in Egypt, when He smote the Egyptians, and delivered our houses." Now as the Israelites were thus taught to observe this service, and to instruct their posterity both in the observance of it, and its meaning; so we Christians have been injoined by Him who is the true Lamb of God, and of whom the paschal Lamb was but a type, ever to observe a service which He ordained, and the meaning of which is given us in the words of the text by one who received it from the Lord Himself. " As often as ye eat this bread, and drink this cup, ye do shew the Lord's death till he come:" and thus as the Israelites, by celebrating their passover, acknowledged the deliverance which God wrought for them, when He smote the first born of Egypt, we, by celebrating the supper of the Lord, acknowledge and commemorate the deliverance from sin and death, obtained for all who would accept it, by the sufferings and death of the Son

of

of God. As long, therefore, as we retain any proper sense of the deliverance thus wrought for us, as long as we entertain any just idea of the salvation thus purchased, so long it might be thought, we should readily join with pleased and grateful hearts in the service ordained for its commemoration. And if, in fact, the present conduct of many Christians wears a different aspect, it may, without injustice, be presumed, that " their love is grown cold," and that they no longer know how to estimate the infinite mercy of God in their redemption, nor the unspeakable love of His Son in becoming a willing ransom for them.

Lest this censure should seem harsh, I will now consider before you, the institution itself, and the end and uses of it, with the obligations thence arising to attend on it: and I am persuaded, from such a review, it will appear, that however the conscientious scruples of some few honest, though weak Christians, who are ever ap-
. prehensive

prehensive of being totally unfit to approach the Lord's table, may plead in their excuse, yet much the greater part of those who absent themselves from it, can set up no defence but what will prove their own criminality.

When our Lord was now about to lay down his life for the sins of the world, and while He was celebrating with His apostles the deliverance which the stock from whence He came, according to the flesh, had experienced in Egypt, He called their attention to a still more important deliverance, even that He was then going to accomplish for all the human race. For taking bread, and having blessed it, He brake it, and gave it unto them, saying, " Take, eat, this is my body, which is given for you." Having taken the cup too, and given thanks, He gave them that likewise, that they all should drink of it, adding, " This is my blood of the New Testament, which is shed for many. This do ye as oft as ye drink it in remembrance of me." Such was the institution

stitution of the Lord's supper, before it had been, by the enthusiasm of some, and craftiness of others, worked up into a tremendous mystery, and adorned with trappings to attract the admiration of the ignorant, and strike terrour into the weak; and if we view it as such, we can never sufficiently admire either its simplicity, its wonderful significance, or that spirit of unexampled love that shines throughout it.

For what could be more plain, what farther removed from all probability of being changed into a superstitious ceremony, than the breaking of bread, and the drinking of wine? Acts which occur every day, and to which, from their so frequently occurring, it was the less likely any particular meaning, but what was expresly declared, should ever be annexed. What requisition could the dying Master have made to his disciples, the compliance with which would have been less burdensome, or less difficult to be continued? While the receiving of the bread and wine does so aptly apply to the thing

for

SERM. VI.

for which it was ordained, a commemorative sign, that the most uninformed follower of Christ cannot but comprehend its significance. Bread is the principal sustenance of human life, the chief support of our bodies; wine is the invigorater of our spirits, the restorer of warmth and chearfulness, after they have been banished by affliction or disease. Is it not then with peculiar propriety that these gifts of Heaven, by which our natural life is chiefly maintained, are made the representatives of that body and blood, by which our spiritual life must be supported, of which, if a man eat and drink, he shall live for ever, and of which, except we do eat and drink, we have no life abiding in us.

Behold a man, whose body is worn by fatigue, and emaciated by fasting, whose spirits are lowered by disease, or oppressed by sorrow; to such an one let the natural refreshments of bread and wine be imparted; his body recovers strength, his spirits revive, his countenance is gladdened: behold the

the sinner deep sunk in guilt and terrour, his love of, and holy confidence in God, changed into sordid fear, his good principles and virtuous inclinations languishing, and his hopes of salvation near expiring; but see such an one washed in the blood of his Saviour, and made partaker of the benefits of his death, the languid flame of piety revives, encouraged by the hope of favourable acceptance, and all necessary assistance, he diligently cultivates every virtuous inclination; and steadily applies himself to the practice of every good work; and daily gathering fresh strength to run the race which is set before him, he aspires after that immortality of which he has here received the earnest.

But the similarity of the effects of our natural and spiritual food is not the only point in which the admirable significance of this sacred institution is apparent; for there prevails in it, too, a most powerful recommendation of that last and new commandment which our Lord, on the same night,

gave

gave to his disciples; that they should love one another.

To partake of the same food, and drink of the same cup, have ever been esteemed tokens of unreserved friendship: and to bring men to spend those hours of ease and frankness together, has generally been thought a great step toward conciliating their minds, and uniting them in the bands of mutual regard. But with how much more reason may we expect the same effects, when the repast of which they partake is made with a peculiar meaning? when all to whom the same bread, and same cup, are communicated, acknowledge by partaking of them, one baptism, one faith, one Lord; confess that the great pursuit of their lives is the same, that their hopes are raised on the same foundation, and their conduct regulated by the same law; and that one great commandment of this law is that which insists on the exercise of universal charity and brotherly love unfeigned? And while the unity of our faith is thus signified,

fied, and the strictness of those bands of affection, in which all the true members of Christ's church are holden together, expressed; the unparalleled love of their Saviour appears, through the same institution, with the fullest lustre; for greater love than this hath no man, that he should lay down his life for his friends; yet when our Lord was about to shew such love, He enhanced the obligation on his disciples, (if it be possible that it could be enhanced) by the manner in which He directed them to commemorate it: no costly sacrifice has He required, no rigorous mortification has He enjoined: to do that only in remembrance of Him which may be of the highest use to ourselves; so to recal to our minds His mercies, as may render us capable of receiving all the benefits of them, and so to keep Him in mind while absent, that we may not be ashamed to meet Him when He shall come again, is the sum of this His precept!

And shall we persuade ourselves that it is a matter of indifference whether we comply with such a precept? Or shall we, like some who call themselves Christians, say the command is spiritual only, and, under that pretence, neglect to obey it? Or shall we not rather, following the dictates of common sense and sober piety towards our Redeemer, endeavour to learn, from the consideration of the ends and uses of the institution, the obligations incumbent on ourselves to observe it?

The apostle tells us, that by this service we shew the Lord's death until He come; that we from time to time recal to our own minds, and testify to others our belief, that Christ suffered for our redemption; that we express the grateful sense we retain of this His love towards us; and testify our firm expectation, that He who already hath appeared in the form of a servant, and patiently borne persecution, misery and contempt, for our sakes, will again appear in glory, to reward with life and happiness eternal,

eternal, those who have obeyed the laws He delivered, and followed the example He set, and to take vengeance on the despisers of His cross, and the enemies of His church.

Now if such be the end of the appointment, if the thus confirming of our faith, and the keeping alive of our gratitude and our hopes be uses of complying with it, (even were they the only ones) How could we neglect to do so, and yet stand excused? Are the mercies of Christ unworthy of remembrance? Is your faith so firm that it needs no additional strength to enable it to repel all the fiery darts of the wicked one? Are the benefits ye have received so deeply infixed in your hearts, that ye want nothing to recal you to a due sense of them? Or is your expectation of your Lord so lively, is your vigilance so great, that ye stand ever prepared to meet Him, and need not be reminded that He is near, even at the doors? But great as these uses are, much as I apprehend we all stand in need of such assistance,

assistance, the confirming of our faith, the keeping alive of our hopes by this act of commemoration, can never be the whole benefit to be derived from duely participating of this holy sacrament. Since our Lord hath said, " He that eateth my flesh, and drinketh my blood, dwelleth in me, and I in him; and as the living Father hath sent me, and I live by the Father, so he that eateth me, even he shall live by me." Words which, when compared with those of the apostle, " the cup of blessing which we bless, Is it not the communion of the blood of Christ: the bread which we break, is it not the communion of the body of Christ?" seem to convey to the true and worthy communicant, who does by faith feed on Him in his heart, and by this act shew forth that faith, a sure promise that the receiving of the bread and wine, of which he partakes, being verily and indeed accompanied by a participation of the body and blood of Christ, which, by these their symbols, he spiritually eateth and drinketh, (and spiritually only it should ever

ever be remembered, according to those words of our Saviour to His disciples, when He had told them that so they must do, " It is the spirit that quickeneth, the flesh profiteth nothing; the words that I speak unto you, they are spirit, and they are life") the participation of them, I say, shall be unto him the means of his becoming, in truth, alive unto righteousness, of his receiving such a portion of the spirit of Christ, as shall enable him to overcome all intemperate passions, and cleanse his heart from all evil inclinations, and prove in him a fountain of piety, holiness, and righteousness: blessed effects, which the goodness and power of God can as well annex to the due and sincere performance of this religious act, as He could cleanse the Syrian from his leprosy, by washing seven times in Jordan!

Let not, then, the plain and simple means by which these great and lasting benefits are conveyed, offend us! but let us rather glorify the wisdom, and acknowledge the love of our Master, who hath, by this one institution so easy of observance, provided for the confirmation of our faith, the conservation of our hopes, the encrease of our piety and holiness, and the improvement of our souls, as well as for preserving, in His church, that bond of peace and charity, in which He hath commanded all who would be truely His disciples, ever to be found. Since, to prevent the Christian, who is rich in this world's goods, from being proud of his opulence, and despising his poor brother, and to preserve this from being stung with envy at the prosperity of the other, What more apt could be devised than inviting both to the same table, where seeing that He who is equally the Lord of both has no respect of persons, they may learn rightly to estimate the present trifling difference that their lots in this world make between them, and as fellow-servants of the same Master, and expecting their last reward from the same hand, chearfully proceed together through the performance of the different tasks allotted them?

Such,

Such, then, being the inſtitution, ſuch the end and uſes for which it was appointed, To what ſhall we aſcribe that very great and criminal neglect of it which is at preſent viſible among us? To ignorance of the command it cannot be imputed; for ſufficiently plain to all is the precept, "Do this in remembrance of me." Neither can the difficulty of compliance be more juſtly alledged, ſince than that nothing can be more eaſy: and I ſhould hope there are none ſo hardy as to eſteem their Saviour's ſufferings unworthy their recollection, or to imagine they ſtand in no need of the aſſiſtance of His Spirit to perfect the work of their ſalvation. To what, then, ſhall we attribute it? in part to want of conſidering the importance of the duty; and in part to a conſciouſneſs of leading ſuch lives as renders them unworthy to join in a ſervice ſo ſacred. To you who have hitherto abſented yourſelves from the former of theſe cauſes, I truſt enough has been already ſaid to convince you of your errour; and for you, who ſenſible of the ſinfulneſs of your conduct,

conduct, thence dare not approach this holy table, let me beseech you to reflect, while ye yet have power to reflect, since ye find ye cannot serve at once Christ and Belial, whose service ye should in wisdom choose? Christ hath commanded you to commemorate His death; this, ye say, the impurity of your lives renders you unworthy to do: but Christ hath also commanded you, to repent and cleanse yourselves from sin. Can your disobedience to this command serve as a plea for your neglect of the other? Or does not your unworthiness, by being voluntary, become criminal also? St. Peter did, on the plea of unworthiness, once hesitate to comply with his Lord's will, in a case, too, in which such hesitation must (if it ever could be so) have been pardonable; But what was our Saviour's judgement of it? "If I wash thee not, thou hast no part with me."

He who instituted the feast is the best judge of the qualifications of those who come to it; and the only one He requires

in

in us is, that we be his disciples, and continue in his words. If we become sincerely such, if we thus live in the true practice of what He hath injoined, the shewing his death by this holy communion, will prove to us a source of comfort inexpressible; for we shall then look for the day of his coming as for that of the arrival of the beloved and gracious Master of the family of which we are members, in whom are placed our hopes of deliverance from whatever evils we may at present feel, and our expectation of peace, security, and perfect happiness. But if our love in this world, if our unwillingness to part with enjoyments that are forbidden, or to practise the self-denial, which religion in some cases requires, induces us to reject the call, and despise the invitation which the Lord hath given us, What will be our confusion of face, when He appears! Think, How shall we then meet Him, with whose request so affectionately made, and accompanied with every circumstance to give it effect, we have thus obstinately refused to comply! What sentence

tence can we then expect from Him? What but the condemnation of those who are lovers of pleasure more than lovers of God, everlasting banishment from the presence of Him whose mercies we have thus contemned, and all the miseries consequent on the wrath of God and the Lamb? Of the power to avoid these, ye are yet possessed; how long ye may continue so, God alone knows; but if ye have any gratitude for the benefits ye have already received, any knowledge of the terrour of the Lord, any care of your own salvation, delay no longer to make use of it; repent and cleanse yourselves from sin; prepare to receive the cup of salvation, and call on the name of the Lord!

SERMON VII.

ON THE LAST JUDGEMENT.

Rev. xx. 12.

And I saw the dead, small and great, stand before God; and the books were opened: and another book was opened, which is the book of life: and the dead were judged out of those things which were written in the books, according to their works.

THE very interesting and most aweful scene, thus revealed by the angel of his Lord to the beloved disciple John, has so manifest a claim to our attention, that it should seem needless to preface a discourse on it with any of the customary exhortations, that ye would seriously listen to the words now

now to be addressed unto you. In subjects on which we sometimes speak, a part only of our hearers may necessarily appear to themselves concerned: with admonitions against theft, and the various acts of dishonesty, those whose opulence removes from them all temptation to such instances of guilt, may think, they have little concern. With dissuasion from oppression, and the abuse of power, those who have none below them over whom they can tyrannize, may conceive, they have nothing to do. But in the judgement which all must undergo, all are interested; and if we consider mankind as distributed under the two great divisions of those, who hope to be acquitted, and those, who fear to be condemned, the latter cannot but be affected with horrour at the mention of that solemn day in which the Son of man, seated on the throne of His glory, shall say unto those on His left hand, " Depart from me, ye accursed, into everlasting fire, prepared for the devil and his angels:" nor the former, without a degree of extasy, anticipate

cipate that hour of triumph, when the King immortal, awarding them crowns of glory, shall say unto those on His right hand, " Come, ye blessed children of my Father, inherit the kingdom prepared for you from the beginning of the world." To encourage these to continue stedfast, immoveable, and always abounding in the work which will secure to each of them that crown which the Lord, the righteous Judge, will give to all that love His appearance, and to raise in those the proper fruits of the fears with which they now look forward to the day of trial, sincere repentance, and timely preparation to meet their God, are the ends of calling their thoughts to that time when " the judgement shall sit, and the books be opened."

It is well known to those who are acquainted with the history of this part of the world, when it was sunk in paganism, that some wise and good men did, in the very nature of things, discover ground of assurance, that men would, after this life,

be

be differently recompensed, according to their works: the Gospel hath fully brought to light the doctrine on which they could form only uncertain conjectures; and confirmed both the hopes and fears of nature, by authoritatively declaring, that " God hath appointed a day in which He will judge the world in righteousness;" and that the concluding act of the dispensations of the Deity, in respect to this globe, will be gathering together all the inhabitants of it, to receive a sentence which shall decide on their future situation, and make it for ever suitable to their conduct past; and the sacred writers strive to impress this expectation on our minds, by mentioning several particulars of the solemn process, represented to us by images taken from human judicatures, and thus justly expressing to our understandings, circumstances, on the natural effect of which on our own minds, we may ourselves determine. Of these circumstances, the principal are included in the text, in speaking to which it is my intention to confine my discourse to the consideration

sideration of what must naturally be the different feelings of the wicked, and of the righteous, when affected by the actual presence of them; not meaning, however, to restrain myself from adverting to other passages of scripture, which may contribute to elucidate any thing but generally mentioned in this.

" And I saw, saith the evangelist, the dead, small and great, stand before God." Our blessed Saviour, in His own description of this solemnity, particularises the glorious train of the Almighty, that innumerable company of angels, which by thousands of thousands minister unto Him. Behold then the assembly, before which ye must one day appear, and without the terrours of guilt to add to his confusion, What man is there among us, that could face such a tribunal, and not be appalled? Consider who will be on the throne; God His self; And will not His excellency make you afraid? While it is difficult to conceive, it is *impossible to describe*, what must then be the terrours;

rours, the diſtreſs, and the anguiſh of the infidel and the blaſphemer, when beholding the brightneſs of His glory, whoſe vengeance they have ſo often dared, whoſe exiſtence they have ſo repeatedly denied, they find themſelves at length really ſummoned to anſwer, face to face, for all the hard ſpeeches they have ſpoken againſt Him.

Here we may well borrow the apoſtle's language, and aſk, If thoſe who obey the Goſpel ſhall then hardly be ſaved, where ſhall the ungodly appear? If ye who have profeſſed Chriſt in the world, who have acknowledged the authority, and joined in the worſhip of God, can only, with trembling hearts, approach His judgement ſeat; if ye who have conſtantly expected, and faithfully waited for it, find this, indeed, the great and the terrible day of the Lord; What will it be to thoſe whom it overtaketh unawares; who believe not its approach, and who now mock at its terrours? On the haughty minds of thoſe ſelf-ſufficient reaſoners,

soners, with whom all faith is prejudice, all devotion superstition, all religion bigotry, the shock produced when they find the sophistry in which they trusted refuted by fact, the belief they rejected justified, the fears they affected to despise realized, must be such as fully to answer that prophetic description given of the extremity of the dismay and confusion of the enemies of God and Christ, in their " saying to the mountains and to the rocks, Fall on us, and hide us from the face of Him that sitteth on the throne, and from the wrath of the Lamb; for the great day of His wrath *is* come, and who shall be able to stand." To the thoughtless hearts of the profligate, who have been wont to treat as dupes all who submit to the restraints of the Gospel, the alarm raised by the awefulness of His visible presence, of whose sanctions and menaces they used to make so light, must exceed, beyond all comparison, the most sudden and the heaviest stroke which disappointment, danger, and affliction in this life, can produce.

Yet horrible as the first sensations of these two descriptions of sinners must be on the disclosure of this tremendous scene, their poignancy must encrease, when they more closely compare the majesty and power of Him before whom they are arraigned, with the insults which they have offered to His dignity, and the disregard they have shewn to His authority. Neither will the crucifiers only of the Saviour of the world then be abashed at looking on Him whom they pierced; confusion of face will also be the just and inevitable portion of all who have rejected, all who have denied, all who have been backward to confess Christ before men: For how will such lift up their eyes to Him, to whom they preferred the favour of the world? When the smile of encouragement, and the clamour of applause, uttered by dissolute companions, shall no more support their confidence? How will those who are wont with profane witticisms, to reflect on the truth, and ridicule the doctrine of Jesus, or even those who, with complacency, listen to these insolent

solent returns of contempt for mercy, and enmity for love, when all being too intent on the wretchedness of their own situation to bestow a thought on others, the number of associates in sin shall cease to embolden, be able to stand in His presence? While, by the lateness of the period at which they are brought to a sense of their guilt, they shall be precluded from even saying with Job, " I have heard of Thee by the hearing of the ear: but now mine eye seeth Thee. Wherefore I abhor myself, and repent in dust and ashes!"

Now although I would hope that no one present has reason to dread the being involved in the condemnation of the unbeliever or the scoffer, yet since it is of much more importance to us to consider, what is likely to befal ourselves, than what others will have to undergo; let me ask, Will it not then, think ye, recur to your minds, that ye yourselves have not, in every instance, manifested love so true, fidelity so sincere, or obedience so constant, as is justly due to

SERM. VII.

so great and so glorious a Master? Will not those trespasses, so inconsistent with humble piety, unfeigned faith, and real love of God, which ye now recollect, and to which I am now endeavouring to awaken your consciences, solely with a view of inducing you to judge yourselves, that ye may not be judged by the Lord, then press themselves upon your mind? Reflect, therefore, in what instances ye have withholden the homage due, in what insulted the Majesty, in what betrayed a backwardness to profess the truth of God; nay, in what even mistrusted His goodness; assured, that His appearance will recal all these things to your remembrance, and thus, at present, take to yourselves a salutary shame for offences, which, if not previously repented of, will, in that day, force shame indelible upon you.

The next particular of the text claiming our consideration, is that of the persons we are to meet before this supreme tribunal; " the dead, small and great:" in whom must

muſt neceſſarily be included all we have injured in any manner, either by perſonal attack or oppreſſion, by robbery or fraud, by calumny or inſult, or even by wilful neglect. All theſe will riſe up in judgement againſt us. And think, if we cannot now meet any one by whom we have dealt harſhly, or to whom we have offered affront without being covered with confuſion, through the conſciouſneſs of our miſconduct, What will be the diſturbance of our minds, when, in the preſence of God and His holy angels, we are at once confronted with all who have juſt cauſe of complaint againſt us!

Here all ranks of men, thoſe of every relation in ſociety, may with propriety, ſhould in charity, be called on to review, with the moſt ſerious impartiality, their paſt conduct, and their preſent habits; to examine themſelves whether they have rendered to all their dues? Whether they continue to owe no man any thing, but to love one another? and if in this their hearts condemn

SERM. VII.

condemn them not, then may they have confidence towards God, and boldness in the day of judgement. But if their love exist only in word or in tongue, and not in deed and in truth, such will their own hearts condemn; And how then shall they appear before Him, Who is greater than our hearts, and knoweth all things? How stand when those who were the objects of their feigned love, have to exhibit against them all the effects of deadly hatred? The general happiness, the good of mankind, are pleas to which we know, from experience, the tyrant and the oppressour are equal; and they are pleas of love. Yet how will these pretenders support their pleas, when all who have been slaughtered through their ambition, all who have suffered by their exactions, all who have been afflicted by their oppression, shall with themselves appear before that judgement-seat, where there will be no respect of persons? Had the wicked only been subjects of their cruelty, yet those unjustly treated would rise again to their confusion; but when

when the harmless victims to their passions, or what is more, when those whom they persecuted for professing the truth, and practising righteousness, for obeying God rather than man, shall present themselves before the throne of the universal Judge, how low then will the loftiest countenance fall; when those by whom they so little expected to be any more disturbed, whom they imagined they had finally crushed, shall, in reality, as the guilty Herod groundlesly fancied of the holy Baptist, be risen from the dead; how will the mighty ones of the earth, who have so abused their power, be covered with astonishment and terrour!

Compared with the total number of the race, few indeed are those, who have the opportunity of making whole nations feel the weight of their power, or the cruelty of their characters; still there are others, who within the limits of their influence or authority, narrow as they may be, are both rigorous and inexorable in their demands

SERM. VII.

on those below them; from whom a defenceless opponent finds no mercy; but who pursue, with unrelenting malice, those who have once incurred their resentment: against those petty tyrants, and other like species of oppressours, who, in sundry ways, take advantage of the unprotected state of the helpless to practise extortion upon them, there are, in holy writ, and especially in the book of Psalms, many appeals to the future judgement of the Lord: when He shall sit to decide on these appeals, and those who, under the justest causes of complaint here, were put to silence, shall meet their Oppressours before His throne, ye will hardly think that the dismay of these latter will prove such as could be too strongly expressed by any words in which I could endeavour to convey an image of it. Pursue the same thought even through more distinct particulars, and ye will thereby gain a juster and a more impressive idea of the horrours with which the guilty and impenitent must necessarily be surrounded in the day of retribution: horrours, from which

which nothing but such repentance as we are conscious is sincere, and firm faith in God for its acceptance, can preserve those who have suffered themselves to become transgressours. Ye are sensible, that even fictitious scenes of divine vengeance will most powerfully affect the human mind; ye know, from experience, that when the tragick poet presents to the murtherer's eyes the apparition of the slaughtered sufferer, even the seeming terrours of the feigned criminal are, to a degree, contagious: from hence, then, ye may partly learn to estimate the distressful sensations of the real murtherer, when he, who the last time he beheld him, was expiring under his relentless hands, shall be called from the grave, and by his very presence pray a sentence from their common Judge.

Let not, however, the approaching situation of the criminals already noticed, dreadful as it is, absorb all your attention; the future feelings of the robber and fraudulent, deservedly claim some of it. For as these,

like

like the former, frequently contract an hardness of heart, which fortifies them against shame and remorse during the whole of their continuance on earth, so must the severity of the shock which they will experience, when this fancied security is suddenly done away by the appearance of those they have wronged before the throne of God, be proportioned to their former obduracy. Numerous are the publick robberies, but still more so are the secret thefts of which the guilty never have, nor in this world ever will be discovered; yet both these combined are outnumbered by the frauds that escape human detection: for the consciences of the criminals remonstrate not loudly enough at present to betray them. Let such, however, recollect, while they are in the way with their adversaries, that unless they now repent, and make reparation, or if this be out of their power, at least do the former with sincerity, when they shall hereafter meet them before an all-seeing Judge, the craft through which they have here lain concealed, the subterfuges

fuges and false pleas by which they now strive to quiet the misgivings of their own hearts, being no longer of avail, the sight of those whom they have pillaged, or on whom they have imposed, will at once harrow up their souls, and put an end for ever to that deceitful calm by which they were lulled to their destruction.

Neither ought the probable sensations of another tribe to be passed over unnoticed; those, I mean, who delight in what may justly be termed the mischief of the tongue. Many are there in the world who suffer in their reputation, in their peace, and in their fortunes, from idle tales, false reports, or malicious suggestions, the authours of which continue unknown, and in numerous cases even unsuspected; but of whom it is almost equally difficult to say, what pleasure they can now find in the wrongs they commit, and the unhappiness they occasion, and what pangs they will feel, when those whose secret enemies they have been, shall with them stand, ready to receive the final sentence

sentence from Him who judgeth rightly! Sufficiently severe ye will undoubtedly conceive, must be the afflicting sense that even these criminals will then have of their own deserts, and of the disgrace and condemnation impending over them: but all consideration of their distressful feelings, will vanish on the mention of those which, in the same hour, will be the portion of others who have employed their speech to still more pernicious purposes; the men, I mean, whose powers of persuasion have been exerted in misleading the ignorant and unwary into transgression, or in seducing the unsuspicious and innocent from the paths of righteousness. When the victims which the nefarious cruelty of such have immolated to their passions, shall, by the agonizing terrours with which they anticipate the sentence due to their own crimes, bear testimony to the deeper guilt of those who caused them to offend, the lashes with which the seducers will then be scourged by their consciences must, ye are sensible, prove such as no comparison drawn from the

the scorpion whips, with which the most inventive poets have armed their feigned ministers of vengeance, can reach; it is inspiration alone that will supply an adequate image, by teaching us to call their sufferings the commencement of everlasting burnings.

Still there is an aggravation that may be added even to the mental sufferings of these; an aggravation which may at first, perhaps, occur to only a few among you; but in your opinion of which, when once mentioned, all will unite: it is in cases where the persons so miserably betrayed to their own ruin, had peculiar claims to the protection of the very wretches that seduced them. This stroke, ye may justly think, carries the picture of human infamy to its utmost height, and, consequently, prognosticates the most acute misery in the breast of the guilty, when the blood of those, who through them perish in their iniquities, is about to be required at their hands. But, alas! for the human race! How great similitude to this transgression is born by conduct that prevails far and wide among us! For are not those betrayed into sin by the very persons who are most strictly bound to guard them against transgression; whose trespasses are owing to the want of the instruction and discipline which their parents have neglected to give them? And are not those, indeed, seduced into it, whom the bad example of their parents has, from their infancy, taught and encouraged to trample on the laws of God? Consider, therefore, while the reflection can produce something more beneficial to yourselves than ineffectual remorse, what anguish will, in that day, pierce the hearts of those parents who receive from their children trembling on the brink of the gulph of everlasting perdition, a glance of reproach, charging them with being the authours of the endless misery into which their unhappy offspring are going to be plunged. Let high and low, rich and poor, listen to the calls thus made on them, to pay every attention that can prevent their children from taking the paths of errour and of vice—let them SERM. no longer prefer fashion to christianity; nor VII. the chance of their success in this world, to the hope of their everlasting happiness in the next. Let not the imbecility of your own minds ruin them by indulgence; much less permit the contagion of your example to draw them from the narrow path of virtue—but check every propensity to these things by recollecting, that the day is approaching, when the guilt of them would draw on you looks of unutterable complaint from those to whom ye have given birth, reproaching you with nothing less than having changed the existence of them who looked up to you as the guides, because ye were the authours of their lives, into an everlasting curse.

Although inexpressible, as ye already perceive, must be the confusion and distress of the guilty arising from the single circumstance of being brought to face all who have just cause of complaint against them, yet we cannot appreciate the wretchedness

of

of their situation as we ought, without taking into consideration the next circumstance mentioned in the text; that of those books being opened, in which the things as yet unknown to the persons against whom they were committed, are contained. But the feelings necessarily to be produced by the certain expectation of such a disclosure, must be considered on some future opportunity. I can detain you no longer at present than to beseech you immediately to turn to that line of conduct, which is prescribed by the knowledge of the circumstances laid before you in the present discourse, " that the Lord hath prepared His seat unto judgement," and that those who sleep in the dust of the earth shall awake. Even while I have been speaking to them, it may possibly have occurred, that in respect to some persons towards whom ye have neglected it, it is no longer in your power to follow our blessed Lord's direction, if thy brother have ought against thee, go first, be reconciled unto him. Let therefore the uncertainty of your being able to make

make reparation for any future trespasses, and your consciousness that it is impossible to do so for some that are past, have their due effects in teaching you caution and humility, that through the former ye may avoid adding to your guilt, and by the latter, deprecate that indignation which your misconduct hath already merited. This admonition is applicable to us all. But for any who may be conscious of any of the more atrocious instances of guilt to which I have alluded, let such take the only method of escaping the misery of which I have been endeavouring to give you an useful, though I could attain to the description of no other than a most inadequate and faint idea; let them follow the example of the holy psalmist, in immediate and sincere repentance; let them call their own ways to remembrance, and make haste, and turn their feet unto the testimonies of the Lord, "Because He cometh, because he cometh to judge the world with righteousness, and the people with His truth."

SERMON VIII.

ON THE LAST JUDGEMENT.

Rev. xx. 12.

And I saw the dead, small and great, stand before God; and the books were opened: and another book was opened, which is the book of life. And the dead were judged out of those things which were written in the books, according to their works.

WHEN I before addressed you on this awful and important subject, I proposed to confine my discourse to an enquiry into, what feelings must naturally be excited in our minds by each of the circumstances, which the evangelist has enumerated in the words of the text; and I accordingly, at that time, proceeded to investigate those which,

SERM. VIII.

which, we must suppose, will arise on finding ourselves arraigned before the throne of God, and confronted with all to whom we have, in this life, given just cause of complaint against us. The next to be considered are the sensations which we must expect to experience on the opening of the records of our conduct: these, indeed, the sinners, with an high hand, those who have learned to make a mock at sin, may defy, as thinking themselves past what they are pleased to call such weakness; but in all others, the very sense of shame justifies a hope of their repentance, and yields encouragement to suppose, that in many breasts serious consideration of what all who will not prepare in time to meet that day, must then undergo, may produce the most beneficial effects.

Suppose yourselves at once, then, in the situation described, the secrets of your hearts going to be disclosed, and God about to judge openly not only all your actions and every word, but the concealed motives of these,

these, those inmost thoughts of your breasts which ye have never ventured even to whisper to a friend. For of all these our blessed Lord and His apostles have assured us we shall render account: "There is nothing covered, that shall not be revealed; neither hid, that shall not be known. Whatsoever ye have spoken in darkness, shall be heard in the light, in the day when God shall judge the secrets of man by Jesus Christ, according to the Gospel."

The certain assurance of such an examination will raise in our minds reflections on the impurity and guilt of the natural man, that will convince us of the absolute necessity of expiation and sanctification by some means far above our own power, and, consequently, dispose us gladly to receive those which God hath been pleased to appoint, the blood of His Son, and the grace of His Holy Spirit; that our sins being blotted out in that day, we may not be partakers of the agonizing feelings then excited by the manifestation of deeds, the perpetrators of of which, by escaping the knowledge of the world, have been misled into a deceitful hope, that their crimes would lie ever concealed. For how will every wretch then, to whose undivulged crimes neither remission has been granted on repentance, nor amendment produced by merciful correction, be seized with terrour at the discovery made of his iniquities! How will those who have encouraged themselves in sin, by saying, " No man shall see us," be confounded, when the volumes of transgression are opened!

Let but each of the guilty recollect what crime it is that he most earnestly wishes to keep concealed from the world, then let him lay it to his heart, that this very fault, of the discovery of which the least danger now fills his breast with tormenting anxiety, shall then be brought to light before the whole assembly of heaven and of earth; and it may be hoped, the anticipated horrours he will feel, will produce the most fervent exertions to prevent, by sincere contrition

trition and real reformation, the actual disgrace and unbounded misery, which will otherwise burst like a tempest upon him.

SERM. VIII.

"The word of God," saith St. Paul, "is quick and powerful, and sharper than any two-edged sword, piercing even to the dividing asunder of soul and spirit, and of the joints and marrow, and is a Discerner of the thoughts and intents of the heart." Now this truth is more especially experienced by us, when those passages of holy writ are repeated, in which mention is made of the last judgement: the word of God then, indeed, directs all our attention to the danger of our own situation, sends us into ourselves, and turns up to our view all those trespasses which lay buried in our hearts under the cares or the pleasures of life. Do not ye yourselves now bear witness to the justice of these assertions? Are not the thoughts of each of you, at this moment, employed on those secret sins which I am warning you God will then set in the light of His countenance? Consider,

there-

therefore, the unpleasantness of your present feelings as but a very slight foretaste of those which await the careless, the obstinate, the impenitent, when deeds now unsuspected shall be proclaimed, authours of mischief now unaccused discovered, and the most mysterious transactions of this life unravelled, and all the actors in them charged with their peculiar guilt.

It is in this world often used as a consolation by the friends of those who have committed any shameful deed, that the disgrace of the culprit will be known only to a few, that industry and caution will prevent the fame of it reaching far—But how short a time will this studied concealment last! the veil which the partial benevolence of earthly friends thus spreads, will, by the justice of the heavenly Judge, quickly be torn asunder! Men much experienced in the ways of the world, are now wont to deem the earth little better than one continued scene of imposition; But what will it appear, then, when to the pretended confidence

fidence of many of the enemies of religion, will be oppofed private acts of a fear worthy to be laughed at; when paft reputation for fanctity, felf-denial, meeknefs, and other virtues, fhall at once vanifh on the difclofure of deeds which fhall leave the guilty no higher honour than that of excelling in diffimulation, and not too, perhaps, without the additional mortification of having themfelves declared the authours of evils, of which they theirfelves entertained no idea, when they ventured on the tranfgreffions that caufed them! Of this, at leaft, I conceive we need have little doubt in regard to that vice which, in the apoftle's phrafe, fets the world on fire, the mifufe of the tongue, when the circumfpection expreffed by, "I would not have it known that I was the perfon who faid it," can no longer be of avail. When the authour of every flander, the wilful propagator of every calumny fhall be dragged to light, when thofe who with mifchievous ingenuity have devifed, and with malicious joy watched over the fuccefs of falfe reports to another's hurt,

hurt, shall, by the records of Heaven, be convicted of these diabolical practices, which they had safely carried on in defiance of human enquiry, their confusion must be such that any attempt to describe it would demonstrate a most inadequate sense of its greatness. For will not all who have by their means been misled, and induced to believe or retail their fictions, all who thereby have been brought to act with distrust or unkindness to those who were falsely accused, all who in any way suffered by the disagreements and contests which their falsities occasioned, stand as appealing against them to Him before whom the false tongue is an abomination?

But if, in such distress the lying lips shall begin to have their reward, What portion of anguish will, at the same hour, seize on the deceitful heart? Of His judgement who knoweth what is in man, not only the actions and the words of His creatures will be subjects, but even their motives; or to speak more correctly, these more especially than

than the former, since, by them alone, the desert of the other can be tried. It can scarcely have escaped your observation, that by the image of our being judged out of those things which are written in the books, is expressed the accuracy with which will be brought to light every circumstance that is necessary to justify, before men and angels, the sentence to be pronounced on the condemned: and in those respecting their motives is particularly contained the guilt of hypocrites. Since their crime consists specifically in pretending other motives for their behaviour than those from which they really act. To how many various species of these criminals the anguish of detection will then reach, it would be difficult to say: for though we most frequently use hypocrisy for a false shew of religious principle, yet it seems by no mean proper to confine it to that; since the enemies of all religion (an host that now appears to encrease daily) assume a love of truth, and desire to free men from the bondage of superstition, as the motives of their conduct. What then will

will be the astonishment of their admirers! What their own confusion! When it shall appear that in reality pride or vanity ruled their hearts, and directed their operations; or that the very righteousness of the law which they opposed, by forbidding the gratification of their passions, made them so adverse to it! How severe must be the mortification of having all the admiration, for which men have in this life been wading through the depths of hypocrisy, suddenly annihilated by its being manifested, that not the motives for which they received so much praise, but others widely different swayed their minds!

Here let the guilty of every kind of insincerity reflect on the disgrace they are preparing for themselves; let not the tribute of applause they now receive for their assumed characters, blind them to their own destruction: let not vain glory cause you to prefer the present praise of man to the approbation of Him who seeth not as man seeth. For how miserable will be the state of of those, who having here oftentatiously displayed their good works, shall then have nothing new to balance all the concealed faults then first disclosed! But far more wretched that of all who, under a fair semblance, have passed through life prosecuting the views of self-interest alone. By discoveries like these will many that are now first then be last, and numbers who before they fell asleep were honoured, will awake to everlasting contempt.

Guilt does, in this world, not only experience great forbearance, but through the prevailing number of culprits, receives no small countenance; but when at the restitution of all things on the side of virtue, there shall appear not only all the righteous sons of Adam, but superiour beings innumerable, headed by Him to Whom all iniquity is abomination, With what sensations will sinners then endure that publication of their vileness, which shall finally stamp their characters in the presence of those who will view them with the most
unequivocal

unequivocal disgust? Recollect, therefore, that how easy soever we may now find it to impose on others, by doing this in any manner, we shall only deceive ourselves more miserably; because a little while, and the frauds practised on them shall be set right; but the effects of these mistakes of our own must be everlasting; for behold, on conviction, sentence is to follow!

The sufferings of mind produced by great disappointment and other severe misfortunes, are such as no man would be willing needlessly to undergo; but compare the greatest misery these can occasion here with the regret, the anguish, and the despair, which must arise on hearing our heavenly Judge decide against us, and the former will appear as nothing. Then will many who now think present enjoyment, or worldly profit, only worth their attention, begin to bewail the folly of their choice, to lament the opportunities they have missed, the happiness they have lost, " We have erred (they will then say) from the way of truth;

truth; we have wearied ourfelves in the way of wickednefs and deftruction. What hath pride profited us? Or what good have riches with our vaunting brought us? All thofe things are paffed away like a fhadow!" When they behold multitudes, which no man can number, come from the eaft, and from the weft, and from the north, and from the fouth, and fit down with Abraham, Ifaac, and Jacob, and all the prophets, in the kingdom of God, and fee themfelves thruft out; think, timely and effectually think, what will then be the torments of their hearts. When in the feparation which our bleffed Saviour hath told us, He will then make among all nations, dividing them as a fhepherd divideth his fheep from his goats, they fee thofe whom they were wont to defpife preferred before them by the unerring judgement of our divine Mafter, when they find the very maxims they ufed to laugh at, the conduct they ufed to ridicule, crowned with the fupreme reward of His approbation, Will they not, when they behold the fervant of God thus exalted, re-

penting

penting and groaning for anguish of spirit, naturally say within themselves, "This was he whom we had sometimes in derision, and a proverb of reproach: we fools accounted his life madness, and his end to be without honour: now is he numbered among the children of God, and his lot is among the saints!"

Far be it from me to exhibit a needless scene of horrour to your minds; but since the day is fast coming on us all, in which we shall necessarily stand in our lot, either on the right or the left hand of the judgement-seat, according to our works, every call to reflection should be used, every topic should be discussed which is likely to prevail on you to prepare to meet your Judge; and therefore, I now put it to your hearts again, Should not yourselves, think ye, in the case just stated, feel the same distress, and make nearly the same reflections that I have repeated? Would not the dread of the punishments to which ye were about to be consigned, overwhelm you with tribulation

lation and anguish? Or could the fearful doom, the irrevocable sentence, "Depart from me ye workers of iniquity into everlasting fire prepared for the devil and his angels," be received but with weeping and gnashing of teeth?

I have, indeed, been hitherto able only to consider one part of the judgement described in the text, that which is calculated to excite in you fear, circumspection, and timely effort to avoid being involved in it— the opening of the book of life, in which may God grant we all may find our names written, (and if we do not it will be our own fault) and the joy attending both the hope and the hearing of our sentence out of that, may hereafter be investigated. For the present I must conclude with exhorting you to let the nearness, and the manifest signs of the approach of this great day, when a new arrangement of men and things will determine our lot for ever, make a beneficial impression on your hearts.

SERM.
VIII.

The interval in which any of us may have it in our power thus to prepare ourselves for judgement, will at most be extended not to many years, while to some but a few remain; and we are all uncertain, whether we may not be called to-morrow, or even to-night; yet come when it will, we know, we must obey the summons. Viewing circumstances in this manner, therefore, to each individual of us our Judge standeth nigh, even at the door. And for the tokens of the coming of that day upon all the inhabitants of the earth, the equity and the mercy of God have provided, ever since He declared His purpose to judge the world, that no generation of Christians should pass without sufficient warning to expect it, the cares and the pleasures of this life may make us inattentive to them, and we may think, that had we lived in earlier ages we should have been so stricken with the signs and wonders then wrought, as to have had our souls alive to the hope of our Lord's return. But as our predecessours in the middle ages were, by having no gain-sayers fayers to disturb their faith, placed on a level with those who went before them, but whose confidence, in the midst of opponents, was supported by recent miracles; so we, by the accumulating testimony of prophecies now rapidly accomplishing in the world, have a light shining on us, sufficient to guide us through all the difficulties, which the prevailing apostacy of the times throws in our way. We have only to be sincere and earnest in making due use of it, then far from our divine Master's coming in a day that we think not of, and in an hour that we are not aware, and giving us a portion with the unbelievers, He will find us watching, and verily we shall be numbered among those blessed servants unto whom He will give a crown of life!

SERMON IX.

ON THE LAST JUDGEMENT.

REV. xx. 12.

And I saw the dead, small and great, stand before God; and the books were opened: and another book was opened, which is the book of life: and the dead were judged out of those things which were written in the books, according to their works.

HAVING already endeavoured, in two discourses on these words, to impress on your minds an effectual sense of the tribulation, anguish and despair, which the circumstances of judgement thus depicted by the evangelist, may naturally be expected to raise in the souls of all, who shall have neglected

SERM. IX.

neglected to lay hold on mercy during the day of falvation; it now remains to call your attention to the more pleafing fcene, which an innumerable company even of fuch as were fometime finners, but have been wafhed, fanctified, and juftified in the name of the Lord Jefus, and by the Spirit of our God, will as neceffarily exhibit through the rapturous feelings of their hearts at the glorious appearance of Him, in Whom, though they have not feen Him, they yet have believed.

Reflection fuggefts, and revelation confirms the fuggeftion, that judgement will overtake us as death found us; I mean that during the intermediate ftate, neither our characters, nor the nature of our expectations, will undergo any change: for as on the one hand, " Repentance in the grave there is none;" fo on the other, " Bleffed are the dead which die in the Lord !" The contraft, therefore, which appears between the finner and the righteous in their laft moments in this ftate, will be continued in the

the next; and by confidering the fenfations of the latter, as directly contrary to thofe of the former, we fhall, perhaps, arrive more nearly than by any other way, at a juft idea of the joy and exultation which they, who love His appearance, will feel, when they fhall awake up after the likenefs of Him, who hath redeemed them out of every kindred, and tongue, and people, and nation.

As aftonifhment, confufion, and terrour, feem the effects to be expected in the breafts of the infidel and the blafphemer, on finding themfelves actually before the throne of their heavenly Judge, fo joy, complacency, and the moft delightful anticipation of permanent fecurity, and encreafing happinefs, will naturally arife in the heart of every faithful fervant on the fight of his divine Mafter. To fay, that human language cannot exprefs the triumphs of that day, is faying but little indeed, fince there is no reflecting mind which will not, on experiment, find all its powers of imagination

tion totally unable to form any satisfactory idea of the exultation which must be the portion of those who have believed, when He who is now gone to prepare a place for them shall, according to His promise, come again in glory, " to take them unto Himself, that where He is there they may be also."

Ye know how much the heart may be elated with imaginary honour, and the false glories of this world; ye are conscious how grateful to the human mind is a victory in any contest, and what self-gratulation arises even from being able to convince an opponent in debate, that the proposition we maintained is right. What then must be the justly-founded raptures of those, who having fought the good fight in this life, and contended for the truth, shall see the palm given to their arguments, and their confidence established, by the sitting of that tribunal, the expectation of which they boldly confessed, and to whose decisions they were wont resolutely to appeal? in lieu of the

the shrieks of dismay then uttered by the enemies of the Gospel, Will not the victorious soldiers of Christ, at this sight, be ready, in triumphant accents, to exclaim, " Lo, this is our God, we have waited for Him, and He will save us: this is the Lord, we have waited for Him, we will be glad, and rejoice in His salvation."

In proportion to the sufferings they passed through for His sake, must be their joy at beholding their Deliverer—the weight of contumely which has been thrown on them, the bitterness of the mortifications they have endured, the severity of the provocations they have withstood, will, according to their measure, all contribute to the encrease of their bliss, on finding that the hour of their redemption is arrived. Then will be understood the saying that is written, " Blessed are they which are persecuted for righteousness sake! And blessed are ye, when men shall revile you, and persecute you, and shall say all manner of evil against you, falsely for my sake!" Then will ye who have been sincere in your obedience to the doctrine of Christ, begin to experience the extensiveness of those blessings which He promised to such as would listen to His words. How the poor in spirit, the mourners, and the meek, can properly be pronounced blessed, will then no longer need explanation; their extasies at the visible presence of Him whose example they endeavoured to follow through sufferings, will prove that their past afflictions were but the seeds of joy. For if the mere ceasing of oppression, be a relief often earnestly wished for; if death be desired as a refuge from the cruelty of men, and the evils of the world, What will be your rejoicing who now suffer for others, or mourn within yourselves, when ye behold Him seated on the throne of power, to whose protection ye have so often commended yourselves, whose promise ye have, that He will wipe away your tears?

Cause enough for the righteous soul to grieve has the world ever yielded, from the shedding

shedding of the blood of Abel to the death of the latest, who have perished in innocence, or the cause of truth; but if ever there were days that more peculiarly excited the feelings of the pious; if ever there were a time in which the enormity of transgressions caused those who hunger, and thirst after righteousness, those who are merciful, and those who are pure in heart, to sigh and look upward, our own are such: from the disgust, then, which ye conceive at the attempts made in these days to eradicate from among men every principle, and every symptom of piety; from the horrours with which ye are stricken at the nefarious mockeries of justice, at the promiscuous and extensive slaughters that have now been perpetrated; from the anguish of spirit with which ye hear the details of the blasphemies, the cruelties, and the impurities in which those who have renounced God and His Christ now glory; Estimate the relief ye will hereafter experience, the joy which will spring in your hearts, the delight which will pervade your breasts,

SERM. IX.

breasts, when ye behold (in the language of the prophet) the Sun of righteousness arise with healing in His wings, and ordering to be gathered out of His kingdom all things which offend, and them which do iniquity, establish that everlasting dominion of His own, which shall never pass away. Neither will ye whose souls are now grieved at dissensions which ye cannot heal; at quarrels and strife, the bitterness of which ye cannot assuage, feel less relief, when ye perceive an end at once put to the wide extended miseries that spring from these, by the appearance of that Prince of peace, of the encrease of whose government there shall be no end.

And thus behold the first part of your future happiness necessarily taking its degree from what ye in this life suffer through your virtues! Go now, and complain of the hard service of religion; murmur at the self-denial which the Gospel prescribes; it forbids, ye may say, the gratification of even natural appetites; it prescribes a sobriety

briety of conduct moſt irkſome to the lovers of pleaſure, moſt intolerable to the votaries of faſhion; harſhly contradictory to the maxims of the world, it treats as of no worth qualities highly eſteemed among men, and inſiſts on practices which invite inſult, and a temper that provokes impoſition: but remember, that this burthen, whatever it be, will to thoſe (and to thoſe only) who endure it to the end, work a far more exceeding weight of glory! Ye may ſhrink from the trial, if ſuch be your choice, but verily thoſe alone who finiſh the courſe can be crowned!

When enquiring into the probable ſenſations of the wicked at the aweful ſeaſon we are conſidering, it appeared, that the more particular we made our inveſtigation, the greater ſeemed the threatened horrours that await them. The contraſt between the impenitent and the righteous will even, in this circumſtance, hold good; for carry on your thoughts to the next particular of the text, that of the perſons who will be aſſembled before

before the judgement-feat of Chrift, and conceive, if ye can, the joy it muft give you at this moft important, and laft needful day, to find a fufficient number around you who would teftify, that when hungry, ye fed; when thirfty, ye gave drink to; when naked, ye cloathed; when ftrangers, ye received; when fick and in prifon, ye vifited thofe, of whom, your Judge has declared, that He will confider fuch good offices done to them, as performed towards Himfelf! Thofe undefcribed fenfations which ye feel on performing acts of benevolence, are, doubtlefsly, attached by our ever-bleffed Creatour to fuch practices, that they may ferve us as incitements to make unto us friends by the Mammon of unrighteoufnefs, that they may receive us into everlafting habitations; and the happinefs with which the confcioufnefs of fuch good works fill your hearts at prefent, ye may well confider as a foretafte, however flight, of the abundant felicity awaiting you, when He, whofe commandment to love your brethren, ye have obeyed, appearing to take account of
His

His servants, ye see yourselves surrounded by such as will bear you witness, that ye have not been barren nor unfruitful in the knowledge of our Lord Jesus Christ.

Listen to the strains in which the great apostle of the Gentiles anticipates the happiness he expected to derive from some, to whom he had been made the minister of good. " For what (saith he) is our hope, our joy, our crown of rejoicing? Are not ye in the presence of our Lord Jesus Christ at His coming? For ye are our glory and joy!" So to all who have been willing instruments of the divine mercy, in ministering to the natural or moral wants of men, whether by relieving the poor, instructing the ignorant, or reclaiming the transgressours, shall the appearance of those to whom they are conscious of having thus performed the task their Lord hath enjoined them, yield joy and glory, when their eyes meeting the grateful looks of those who, by their well-timed bounty, were preserved from giving way to temptations to dishonesty
that

that then pressed sore upon them, or by their lessons were delivered from the deceitfulness of errour, and all the dreadful consequences of impious maxims, or by their friendly warnings and earnest admonitions, converted from sin unto righteousness, shall, from the humble confidence of their countenances, inform them of the blessed effects of their charitable exertions. What exultation, what a crown of rejoicing, will they not then find in works, which, though here perhaps little noticed, have followed them to the throne of judgement! And if such kindness to whom ever exercised, shall then whisper peace and joy to your souls, where it has produced its intended effects on those to whom we are more nearly related in the flesh, Will not the knowledge of them raise sensations directly opposite to the anguish and the horrour which await the negligent parent, and the faithless guardian? Will not ye who have taught your children and your housholds to keep the way of the Lord, and to do justice and judgement, who have endeavoured to infuse into their hearts

hearts not the love of the world, but the love of God, and directed their attention beyond thofe which are feen, to the things which are not feen, in that hour rejoice with joy unfpeakable, and full of glory, over thofe whom ye yourfelves directed to the path of life?

Rapturous, indeed, will be the feelings fpringing from this fource, yet muft they receive encreafe from the next fucceeding circumftance in this great procefs, the opening of the books; by which the characters of the righteous will be cleared not only from the reflections of the invidious, and the mifreprefentations of the malicious, but from the degrading, though groundlefs imputations, of the ignorant and the foolifh, who, under the proud affectation of pity, often cenfure conduct, of which the motives are fufficiently exalted, to be far above out of their fight.

The victories of the righteous are chiefly gained over himfelf, and, confequently, make

make neither noise or appearance in the world, though the measures necessary to them may often require a conduct, to which the dissolute or the thoughtless will readily apply the opprobrious terms of unsocial, niggardly, and spiritless. But be of good courage, ye who seek not the praise of men; the less known to the world your present labours are, the greater shall be your glory before the throne of Him in whose sight ye wish to stand approved; your heavenly Father Who seeth in secret, will reward you openly: and "when the book of life is opened, with great boldness will ye stand before the face of such as afflicted you, and made no account of your labours!" Often, in the anguish of your souls, have ye appealed to the judgement of your God, for the innocence of your conduct, for the rectitude of your intentions; often complained of the cruelty of the suspicions entertained, and of the slanders uttered against you; how your words have been misinterpreted, your deeds misrepresented, and your good evil spoken of; but behold the hour cometh,

cometh, when for all your griefs, ye shall receive more than double, at the hand of Him who judgeth rightly! Think, what will then be your joy, when you receive the authoritative affurance, that the end ye fought in all labours is fecure! What your ecftafy on hearing your names announced among thofe that are written in Heaven! We know from numerous examples, that tidings of great joy can excite fenfations fo exquifitely great, as in our prefent frame cannot even be fupported; What then fhall we think of the feelings of thofe who, without fainting under it, will experience a happinefs to which the higheft this ftate can yield, will bear no comparifon!

And yet great, inconceivably great, as this muft be, judge ye, whether it will not be augmented by hearing any whom we have loved in this ftate, called to the fame happy lot. Neither entertain in your hearts any mifgivings that the enjoyments of the righteous from the laft circumftance, will be at all counterbalanced by their forrow for

for those whom, having here regarded, they shall perceive are consigned to a different doom. The pious, indeed, are not used to be intimately connected with those whom they know to be ungodly, the number of such cases will, therefore, be by this mean reduced; and where they have unwittingly contracted a personal affection for them, the vileness then manifested in the condemned, will in the spirits of just men made perfect, raise an abhorrence of their characters, which will at once extinguish all affection, and make them acquiesce, without reluctance, in the justice of their sentence.

Should it farther suggest itself to you, that in a disclosure of conduct so general, even of the best men many things must be revealed of which they will then be ashamed, and hence your hopes of unmixed happiness be lessened. Attend to the particular language of the text; "And another book was opened, which is the book of life." As if it had been said, the secret deeds of the wicked, indeed, shall be brought to light, to prove the juftice of their condemnation, but the naming of the good, as the chofen of God, will be a fufficient teftimony of their worth, while their tranfgreffions of which they have truly repented, fhall not be called to remembrance, according to the word of the Lord by the prophet Ezekiel, " If the wicked turn from his fin, and do that which is lawful and right; if the wicked reftore the pledge, give again that he hath robbed, walking in the ftatutes of life without committing iniquity, he fhall furely live, he fhall not die. None of his fins that he hath committed fhall be mentioned unto him." Unabafhed, therefore, by the repetition of tranfgreffions already blotted out, having wafhed their robes, and made them white in the blood of the Lamb; with enlightened minds and rectified attachments will they be prepared to tafte, with unmixed enjoyment, the felicity which will arife from feeing in the feparation that the great Shepherd of the flock fhall then make, thofe whofe fouls were in this life moft congenial with their own, placed with them-

themselves on the right hand; and from anticipating the blifs of the endlefs ages of promifed happinefs, on which they are now about to enter in the company of thofe with whom they once parted in all the bitternefs of grief, but from whom they fhall henceforth never be feparated. Raife then, as nearly as ye can, your hearts to an idea of this fituation, when ye fhall ftand, expecting from the mouth of Him who died that ye might live, but who liveth for ever and ever, thefe words, decifive of everlafting felicity, " Come, ye bleffed children of my Father, receive the kingdom prepared for you from the beginning of the world." And confider, whether the hope of partaking in this lot, at the end of our days, be to be relinquifhed for the fake of any enjoyments we can now have, or through fear of any exertions that may be now neceffary—the heart of man, indeed, cannot conceive the good things which God hath prepared them that love him; but confider only the happinefs which in this world is provided for the human race, if

fin

sin had not come in and interrupted the enjoyment of it; reflect with how great sincerity yourselves and others have exclaimed, How happy could we be but for such and such circumstances, all of which arise from sin in itself, or its consequences; and ye will then so apprehend the peace and joys of that state, in which there shall be no more curse, no more death, neither sorrow, nor crying, nor any more pain, as may excite you to set your affections on things above, to run so that ye may obtain, and now, *indeed* putting away every thing unworthy a candidate for Heaven, gain for yourselves, though an humble, yet a most joyful confidence, that when the judgement shall sit, and the books be opened, ye shall receive the command to take possession of the inheritance of the sons of God, and to enter into life!

SERMON X.

ON THE FUTURE STATE OF HAPPINESS.

Rev. XXI. 1.

And I saw a new heaven and a new earth.

VARIOUS particulars of that glorious inheritance, to which all Christians are taught to look as the sure reward of their faith and obedience, are mentioned in other parts of the sacred writings; but in the two concluding chapters of the Revelation vouchsafed to the beloved disciple, and through him given to the church, they are all placed in one point of view; and the recovery of fallen man from transgression, from the curse and death, and his restoration to those blessings, which were forfeited

by

by the sin of our first parents, the tree of life, and the presence of God, are by the spirit of prophecy openly declared. And thus are these Holy Scriptures, though consisting of so many different portions, written by various persons, in ages and places widely distant, closed in a manner accurately corresponding with their beginning: and the account they give us of God's dealings with the human race, is rendered complete, by being carried on to that time when, through the omnipotence of their Creatour's mercy, they shall be restored to the secure possession of that state of happiness, in which He had placed them, when they were first called into being.

Few persons, I conceive, read with attention the second chapter of Genesis, without regretting the loss of that paradise, which the Lord had planted; or without (on comparing the happy life which the descendants of Adam might there have passed, with their present situation, in the midst of frailty, pain, and sorrow) being, led

led to wish for that restoration of all things, with an intimation of which the Lord God was pleased to alleviate the sentence He pronounced on His disobedient creatures. Now the gratification of such a wish, in its fullest extent, is displayed to us in the vision of the text; and which I have chosen for subject of discourse, because the particulars therein revealed are calculated, not only to excite in our minds the most earnest desires to be admitted to a state so full of glory and happiness, but to convince us also of the indispensable necessity of those preparations, which the Gospel, in almost every page, warns us to make against the appearance of that kingdom. May I not therefore hope, that the attention to this subject will be as general as the interest we have in it, and earnest in proportion to the loss with which deficiency on our part would be attended?

Now, although the representation which this vision contains of the glories of the heavenly Jerusalem, (called heavenly, because

SERM. X.

cause it comes down from Heaven) be evident, for the most part emblematical, though they be described under the images of those things which at present convey to our minds the highest ideas of pure magnificence, and unclouded splendour; yet several of the blessings to be inherited on the new earth are literally expressed, while even those that are conveyed in figure, are not so darkly shaded, but that we may form notions of them sufficiently clear and strong, to raise in our breasts most anxious desires to be thought worthy of admission to them. If they are not designed to be contemplated by us, What reason can be given for their having been revealed? Since these cannot, like other parts of the line of prophecy, be of service, when they are fulfilled, as testimonies of the truth of revelation; because when the day of judgement is once arrived, no further demonstration will be wanting. The end, therefore, of such delineations of particulars of the future state, must be to arrest our attention, and to render us desirous of partaking of the good things

things thus set before us in similitudes. And if so, surely it is not dealing fairly by ourselves, not to make use of the means thus afforded us of engaging our affections on the side of our real interest. We know that the preference men give to the things of this life, arises not from any superiority they are even supposed to possess over those of the next, but merely from their being present: to counteract, then, the effects of a circumstance, which experience shews to be so powerful, we may, by the use of reflection, place the future blessings in a light so strong before our minds, as to make the deepest impressions on them; and if we neglect to use the power we thus possess of fixing our inclinations on things eternal, Who but ourselves will in justice be to blame for all the consequences of our thus acting against the dictates of common sense? Under this consideration let us proceed to a brief review of the particulars mentioned in this most aweful and interesting part of revelation.

The

SERM. X.

The first more remarkable circumstance that occurs in the apostle's account of the new earth, is, that on it " there will be no sea." A point well worthy of attention, on account of its perfect consistency with that state of happiness we are taught will be there enjoyed. For of that commercial intercourse which is now carried on by means of the great body of waters, and which conveys the products of one country to supply the wants of another, there can be no need in a state in which the infirmities and the necessities of the present shall be no longer known. Neither will other purposes to which the ocean has here contributed, by keeping nations separate for ages, exist in a world, where the whole dispensation is complete, and not, as in the present, only in progress to something hereafter to be revealed. Severe, and many are the evils caused by the sea; the prospect it yields, however grand and striking on the first view, is, in fact, a barren prospect, and full of melancholy suggestions. If an ocean be subject to storms, it must occasion afflictions;

afflictions; and could we suppose it always free from them, it must produce exhalations the most noxious and disgusting. So that in every view taken of it by man, (and, let it be remembered, it is to man that the prospect of happiness in another world is intended to be given in the Gospel) the sea is a part of the globe he lives on, incompatible with the perfect happiness of its inhabitants, and which, consequently, it might justly be expected, would no longer exist where such happiness is to be enjoyed: in exact conformity to which expectation, excited by reasoning on the very nature of things, St. John declares, that on the new earth he saw " there was no sea."

In the state from which will thus be banished, what is a source of so many and severe sufferings in the present, " There shall (it was farther revealed to the apostle) be no more death, neither sorrow, nor crying; neither shall there be any more pain." And thus will the sons of Adam be freed from all the afflictions under which they at

present

present groan; with this peculiarity in their state of relief, that there will be room to dread any alteration of it. Here the certainty of death, and the uncertainty of its season, render even in the youngest the entertainment of sanguine hopes of any distant enjoyment, a subject of reproof, an object of ridicule; but there ye may plan future schemes of happiness without danger of disappointment, and engage in the longest pursuits without hazard of interruption. Doubt will then give way to security, and hope be changed into possession. The sigh of mourning, the lamentation of disappointment, the complaint of oppression, and the shriek of terrour, will then no more be heard; because "the former things are passed away:" but safety unmenaced, joy unalloyed, happiness unmixed, will be to those who are deemed worthy of an entrance into that state, because "the Lord God hath made all things new."

But the particular more circumstantially noticed in this portion of the vision, is "the

"the great city, the Holy Jerusalem," described as composed of materials which plainly allude to those characters of which its citizens will consist. The Lord had promised, by the prophet Zechariah, to try the remnant of Israel as the gold is tried; and thus St. John declares, that the city was of pure gold. By the mouth of the prophet Malachi it was said likewise, that those who feared the Lord, and thought upon His name, should be His in the day when He made up His jewels: to this allusion how strongly answers the figurative description of the heavenly Jerusalem: the building of the wall is of jasper, its foundations are garnished with all manner of precious stones, and the twelve gates are twelve pearls. In consistency with other scriptures on the foundations, are inscribed the names of the twelve apostles; and as entrance into this holy city is accorded only to those who are engrafted into the stock of Israel, on the twelve gates are the names of the twelve tribes of the chosen people. While the number of its square measure exactly

exactly anſwers to the number of that glorious company, which are declared to be the "firſt-fruits unto God and to the Lamb." In the midſt of this community are found the trees of life, and the river of life: and to complete the glory of the ſcene, the throne of God and the Lamb ſhall be in it; and "His ſervants ſhall ſee His face."

Now what a ſubject for reflection, what an object of earneſt deſire, is here preſented to our minds, in the happineſs to be enjoyed in a world from which every natural inconvenience, every moral evil, will be everlaſtingly baniſhed; and the citizens of whoſe capital will be ſpecifically the congregation of the very beſt men that have paſſed through this life, purified even from the few imperfections they betrayed under the ſevereſt trials of the preſent world; and placed by the unerring ſentence of the Judge of all the earth, in their proper ſtation, at the head of human kind! For into this city, it is declared, "they ſhall bring the glory

glory and the honour of the nations." And, indeed, to dwell round the throne of the Almighty, and be appointed to refide under the immediate glory of His vifible prefence, is a diftinction, which raifes a creature to a degree of exaltation, which not the generality of fons of Adam alone, but, perhaps, ftill fuperiour beings, may look up to, while theirfelves move only in a lower fphere. But " Will God, indeed, dwell with men?" and Can an inheritance like this be referved for fuch unprofitable fervants? Thefe are queftions of wonder which, while they naturally arife from reflecting on the immeafurable diftance between our heavenly Father and ourfelves, lead alfo to the confideration of the indifpenfable neceffity there is for thofe preparations which the Gofpel fo earneftly and fo repeatedly warns us to make againft the appearance of the kingdom of Heaven. For if the good things which revelation thus declares, God hath prepared for thofe who love Him, be fo excellent, that it is abfolutely an exercife of our faith to perfuade suade ourselves of the possibility of the gift; how much less can we believe, that any share in them will be granted to those, who refuse to comply with the conditions on which they are offered; or neglect to obtain the qualifications, which are declared requisite in every one, who shall partake of them? If ye are astonished, that God should in any wise condescend to dwell with men; ye cannot be surprized that He should require those of them, among whom He will vouchsafe to dwell, to purify themselves as He is pure. The very fact of God's purposing to exalt all the followers of Christ to such glory, accounts at once for the charge given to all who name the name of Christ to depart from evil; and proves, that by the strictness of the Gospel precepts, it is not merely the exercise of our faith, or the trial of obedience, that is intended; but the rendering us such characters, as are requisite to fill that high station, to which the goodness of God, through Christ, will promote those among us, who choose to qualify themselves for it.

Hence-

Henceforth then, when ye find yourfelves inclined to complain of the purity which the Gofpel requires in its difciples, take into the account the holinefs of that community, of which thefe difciples are admitted probationary members; and afk yourfelves, whether any characters fhort of thofe which we are required to become, would be fit to be exalted to a ftation fo dignified, fo glorious, as that declared to be referved for the real followers of Chrift. When ye would foothe yourfelves under the remembrance of your tranfgreffions, and proceeding in all the cant of the reprobate, ye argue, that furely the divine mercy will never require this commiffion, and that neglect, at the hands of fo frail a creature as man; recollect, that the determinate connection between righteoufnefs and happinefs is already eftablifhed by the nature God was pleafed to give to things, when in the beginning He created them. Confiftently with which we find our bleffed Lord mentioning the kingdom to be inherited by thofe of whom He fhall approve, as prepared for them from the beginning of the world. Proceeding then on these facts; that without holiness, no man shall see the Lord; and that this holiness is a real character, to which alone are adjusted the glories and the enjoyments, the honour and the happiness of the future state: consider the absolute necessity of acquiring this holiness, if ye wish to be succesful candidates for a portion among the sons of God. Or should ye imagine, that a less perfect righteousness might save you from condemnation; and provided that point be secured, be content to give up the highest glory to which ye are called; (for to what will not the meanness of vice submit) recollect, that the composition ye wish for is not to be made; for it is declared, that those very characters who, on account of the defilement they have contracted, shall not enter into the holy city, shall moreover have their part in the lake which burneth with fire and brimstone. And need ye be told the reason of the condemnation of such characters? Or is it not manifest to any one, who will be

at

at the pains of thinking at all seriously on this most important of all subjects, that as they who have not obtained habits of purity, charity, and piety, would both be uneasy in themselves, if placed in a society so holy, and also offend others by the irregularity of their behaviour, thus interrupting the promised tranquility of that happy state; so men, who have rejected the mercy of God, despised His promises, and thought scorn of that heavenly country, are presumptuous transgressours, the guilt of whose disobedience being estimated by their obligations to attention, is sufficiently great to merit all the punishments with which these scriptures threaten the impenitent?

From this untoward generation, therefore, it is yours to save yourselves. The question which was put to the children of Israel, in the name of the Lord, may with justice be put to the church of the Gentiles likewise; " What could have been done more to my vineyard, that I have not done in it?" On the first preaching of christianity,

anity, a doctor of the Jews, celebrated for his learning, his abilities, and his character, not yet convinced of the truth of the Gospel, stated what he considered as a decisive test of its coming from Heaven. "If this counsel, or this work, be of men, (said he) it will come to nought. But if it be of God, ye cannot overthrow it." And this test was so far assented to by its most bitter enemies, who had opportunity of examining on the spot the pretensions and the works of its preachers, who were well versed in the doctrines on which it was founded, and in possession of the Scriptures on which it claimed, that they for a season withheld their hands, then stretched out in persecution of its professors, but finding that it stood the test proposed, and that instead of decreasing in its influence, it wonderfully grew and prospered; they renewed their cruel efforts to extinguish it, but though still more potent enemies joined in the attempt, after a period of upwards of 1700 years, here are we inhabitants of a far distant region of the earth, assembled in acknowledgement of the divine origin of that Gospel, which (Gamaliel well argued) would, had it not been of God, have come to nought.

In addition too to this constant call made on us to be mindful of the reality of that system of divine government under which we live, from the hour of its being first preached to the present instant, the situation of the professors of the Gospel have been accurately such as was pre-signified by the prophets, the apostles, and the Lord Himself—the sins of christendom have, in fact, been visited, and the corruptions of christianity avenged, until, in the present age, the want of consideration of the judgements of God, and indifference to His approbation or His wrath, being become almost as great and as general as they can be, His inflictions begin to assume an appearance more terrifick than has yet been seen. Instances of nations apostatizing from christianity, instances of their most grosly corrupting its doctrines and perverting its precepts,

and

and of the divine judgements falling on them for thefe things, and of their confequently finking from a high ftate of civilization into the loweft barbarifm, ye may perhaps find recorded in hiftory. But that of a very numerous nation, among whom learning had long been cultivated, the arts and fciences had long flourifhed, and which had, as it were, fafcinated all its neighbours into a fervile imitation of its follies and vices, formally renouncing the Gofpel, abolifhing, by order of a government in which they all affected to participate, the obfervation of the Lord's day, and fhutting up their churches; and moreover, deliberately forming plans for continuing infidelity and vice to fucceeding generations among themfelves, and propagating them in furrounding nations, and from the moft polifhed, becoming, in an inftant, as it were, the moft favage people on the earth: while the inhabitants of the adjoining lands (not even excepting our own) appear to be much lefs averfe to their principles than fearful of their arms, is a novel occurrence unparalleled

unparalleled in the annals of mankind, yet forming an actual commencement, and indicating the future growth of such a darkness as it is written, shall in the last days cover the people; when, instead of making the proper use of their sufferings, and repenting of their deeds, they shall only blaspheme the God of Heaven because of their pains and their sores: and thus manifest to us, that we are not indeed far removed from the last link in that chain of events which the scriptures have described to us, as extending from the time of our blessed Saviour's ascension to Heaven, to that of His coming again. Is this a time, then, to be thoughtless of our salvation, when the day, that must bring forth the sentence of it, is so plainly near at hand? Or, is the hope of the scene of happiness I have this day set before you from the Scriptures, not worth cherishing? For if it be deserving of any attention, it must be so of the highest.

SERM. X.

In the name of God, therefore, of that God who offers you such inexpressible mercies, let me beseech you to make a real and effectual use of the light of His revelation while ye yet have it; it may in wrath, it will in judgement, be taken from those who refuse to walk by it. That this has before been done, ye see in the fate of His ancient people the Jews; ye see it in what has befallen many who once called themselves Christians. And should ye, by your wilful deafness to this and every call, bring down the same sentence on yourselves, What, can ye conceive, will be the regret, the horrour, the anguish of your souls, when waking in another life, and seeing the promised glories of the sons of God revealed, ye are told that your portion lies another way! Ponder well this question: and recollecting that the kingdom of Heaven consisteth not in *words*, any more than in *meat* or *drink*, strive to obtain an inheritance therein, by both holding fast the faith, and practising the works of a Christian; referring constantly to the Testament of your Lord,

Lord, that ye may know what is truly the work He hath left you to do; and frequently reviewing His promises, that ye may rise superiour to every difficulty, and be carried triumphantly through every trial, by the blessed hope of being, in the end, admitted " to the city of the living God, the heavenly Jerusalem, and to an innumerable company of angels, to the general assembly and church of the first born, which are written in Heaven, and to God the Judge of all, and to the spirits of just men made perfect, and to Jesus the Mediatour of the new covenant." To Whom with Him that sitteth upon the throne, be ascribed, as is most due, salvation and blessing, and glory, and wisdom, and thanksgiving, and honour, and power, and might; for ever and ever!

SERMON XI.

ON THE FUTURE PUNISHMENT OF THE WICKED.

St. Matt. xxv. 46.

And these shall go away into everlasting Punishment.

THE particular earnestness with which our blessed Lord warned men of the fearful doom awaiting the wicked, accurately corresponds with the character of Him, who came to be, through his own sufferings, the Saviour of all, who are willing to be saved from such condemnation. In a discourse recorded in the latter part of the ninth chapter of St. Mark's Gospel, he repeated no less than three several

several times the images under which he was wont to describe the torments of the cursed. But this earnestness does, on the other hand, as little accord with the imagination that the menaces of a fire which never goeth out, and a worm which never dieth, are, in great part, but empty threats: a presumptuous and silly conceit, which some corrupters of the Gospel strongly support, while others, who unfeignedly loath any participation in their guilt, take it up under a mistaken notion of its tending to manifest the glory of God and of Christ.

Great as are the punishments threatened to the wicked, it is plain the prospect of them does not intimidate men from the practice of sin; and the menaces, consequently, are not greater than are absolutely requisite to deter men from the breach of the divine laws. But if human perverseness be such, as to demand menaces of punishments so severe, should those menaces be despised, will justice require any thing less than the absolute infliction of the penalty threat-

threatened? In support of the negative of this question it has been argued, that the sanctions of the divine law, it must be presumed, will be perfect; but as that to which any thing can be added is not so, it necessarily follows, that the penalties on the breach of that law must be everlasting.

In reply to all these reasonings, not only the mercy of God is pleaded, but it is even pretended, that such retribution would be matter of injustice; and thus is the dread of future punishment lessened, and sanctions, which already prove in many cases of no avail, reduced to be ineffectual in still more. To prevent ourselves from being misled, nay, cheated of our salvation, by the shallow but presumptuous blessings of either those who wilfully oppose the truth, or others who are deceived by the plausible cloak of tenderness for the infirmities, and pity for the sufferings of men; let us now examine the arguments of those who would persuade us that the punishment of sinners will not be everlasting; and then proceed to

SERM. to consider the miseries of that lot, which
XI. reason suggests, and scripture declares, will
be their portion in another state.

The first topick from which these reasoners argue, is the divine mercy, with which they say, it is inconsistent to have created beings who would make themselves everlastingly miserable. But surely, when contemplating the perfections of our Creatour, we are bound to enquire with caution, and pronounce with humility. Whatever may be our future lot, that it was not inconsistent with His goodness to make us subject unto it, is manifest from our existence itself; and how far His mercy will extend to affect that lot, He certainly must best know. If we have, then, a revelation of His will concerning it, the words of that must be decisive; and it is absurd to look out for any other ground on which to form our expectations concerning it. Since if we discover something that may encourage us to draw a conclusion different from what is revealed, and lead us to imagine

that

that we thereby exalt the mercy of our God; we shall still be doing this at the expence of His truth. If God hath declared in His Gospel, that the wicked shall go into everlasting punishment, all our speculations on His mercy will prove nothing but our dread of such a doom, as long as His truth must stand unimpeached.

In the same manner may be answered the arguments which the same reasoners draw from the perfection of the satisfaction made by the sufferings of Christ. That will, doubtlesly, reach to all for whom He will intercede: and therefore, in part perhaps, is all judgement committed unto Him; that He may exercise the most uncontrouled power of salvation. Still hath He declared by His apostle, that He gave Himself for us, that He might purify unto Himself a peculiar people: still has He taught in His own person, that strait is the gate, and narrow is the way, that leadeth unto life, and few there be that find it; and still has He commanded His disciples to go, and preach

SERM. XI. preach to all nations, that he that believes, and is baptized, shall be saved; and he that believeth not, shall be damned. And still has He affirmed, that He will, in the last day, say unto those on His left hand, " Depart *from me*, ye cursed, into everlasting fire, prepared for the devil and his angels."

To avoid the force of this last text, and others of like meaning, we are sometimes boldly assured, that the word rendered everlasting, should not be so understood. Yet is the same term used to express the never-failing existence of God Himself, as in the sixteenth chapter of the epistle to the Romans, " according to the commandment of the everlasting God." And this very evasion seems to be guarded against in the Scriptures, not only by the circumlocutions employed on this head, when the place of torment is described, as that where their worm dieth not, and their fire is not quenched: but by its having been specifically declared, that the bodies of the dead

shall

shall be raised incorruptible; and each of the future states shall be unchangeable. In the former of these points, we are instructed by St. Paul, in the fifteenth chapter of his first epistle to the Corinthians; and the last our Lord hath taught us in the parable of the rich man and Lazarus. Now surely, if the subjects of punishment be to exist for ever, and yet, when once placed in the torments to which they are condemned, never change their state, it must be something more than folly to deny, that their punishment shall be everlasting.

But by others it is affirmed, that such a dispensation would be unjust, and therefore we must be mistaken in our deductions from Scripture; and that, because there is no proportion between temporal offences and eternal punishment. Now this observation would be just, if the guilt of an offence were always in proportion to the time employed in the commission of it; but far from this, a trifling imposition may require many days for the accomplishment

SERM. XI.

of it; while the horrid crime of murder may be committed in a moment. Duely to eftimate the criminality of a tranfgreffion, the obligation we are under to obey the law tranfgreffed, muft be taken into confideration: and our obligations to comply with the divine commandments are infinite; the guilt contracted by the breach of them muft therefore be the fame; and, confequently, if juftice require (as thefe reafoners theirfelves contend it does) that the punifhment be in proportion to the crime, the punifhment attached to tranfgreffions againft God muft be infinite. Neither fhould it be fuffered to pafs unobferved, that the fins of the impenitent do, in fact, continue as long as they are capable of tranfgreffing; and would (fince we may be certain the divine mercy denies to no man, who would make ufe of it, opportunity for repentance) proceed infinitely, were they not ftopped by the intervention of death. So that although their actual crimes may be numbered, the wickednefs of their hearts feems paft all eftimate:

and

and that the punishment of such souls should be the same, cannot be matter of injustice.

To return then to the declarations of scripture as unaffected by exceptions so vain; the duration of the punishment of sinners is expressed in the very same terms as that of the happiness of the righteous: and the variation of phrase introduced by our translators in the last verse of the chapter of the text, " and these shall go into everlasting punishment: but the righteous into life eternal," is totally unwarranted by the original. If the sufferings of the former, therefore, are to be but temporary, neither are the joys of the latter; and thus is the glory of the Christian dispensation eclipsed, the endless ages of happiness procured, by the blood of Christ, for those whom He hath redeemed out of every kindred and tongue, and people and nation, reduced to a limited period of enjoyment, by the fantastical speculations of vain men; who, though they may not see this consequence

SERM. XI.

of the tenet they have embraced, could, one should think, if they first investigated it as they ought to do, scarcely fail of perceiving, that by asserting a temporary punishment for sinners, they are introducing again one of the mischievous errours of the church of Rome, the long-exploded doctrine of purgatory.

Having thus cleared our way through the difficulties started against the doctrine of the text, by the fears rather than the reason of men, it remains to consider the miseries which, in another state, await those who will not use the opportunity for repentance which this affords.

That which is so commonly said of the terrours which great sinners sometimes manifest on their death-beds, that they already suffer the torments of the damned, may well suggest to us the first portion of those miseries, into which the impenitent must hereafter sink. For as their last sufferings here proceed from dread of the punish-

punishment justly due to their crimes, and from remorse at having wasted their time and their faculties on things which profit not, we may most reasonably conclude, that the same fears, and the same self-reproach, will keep possession of their souls when separate from their bodies. And when these are encreased by the reflection, that the day of salvation is entirely past, and when no external objects remain to divert the thoughts, or relieve the attention, even for a moment, from the tremendous prospect, their sufferings, even during this period of them, will be such, as to make them think, whatever they have gained in this world by their transgressions, much too dearly purchased.

But when the hour of sentence arrives, what was before only the effect of fear, must be advanced into the result of certainty; and the being marked by the decree of that Judge who cannot err, with the character of one fit to consort only with the devil and his angels, will naturally occasion

casion a degree of mortification, give rise to such an height of terrour, as no words can express, no imagination at present reach. Neither will this mortification be transient, or these terrours vain, since the former will be rendered permanent, and the latter realized, by an everlasting separation from the congregation of the righteous, and perpetual banishment from the presence of God. And now, for the purpose of exciting yourselves to every possible exertion for avoiding such a doom, conceive, as far as ye can, what would be the feelings of your souls under it. Having, from the sentence of approbation with which they were honoured in your presence, caught a glimpse of the glory which the righteous inherit, What would be your regret on reflecting, that you had presumptuously despised the offer, madly neglected the opportunity of obtaining the same! In alleviation of the mortification of disappointment, and the pains of grief, we here often successfully recur to scenes of festivity, or the conversation of those who are at ease; and great is the relief

lief we thus obtain. But when all around us are as wretched as ourselves, and the whole region to which we are banished, resounds with the cries of lamentation, and the groans of despair, no intermission of sorrow, no cessation of misery, will be within our reach. The methods which we here have taken to stifle the rebukes of conscience, and render ourselves insensible to the voice of truth, will then appear the most cruel deceptions; and our sufferings, instead of being diminished by communication with those who could pity and relieve, must be rather encreased by being imparted to the wicked in despair: while the hour of repentance, which here rather soothes the soul of the sinner who is brought to a sense of his offences, being past, for contrition, obduracy alone remains; and that love of God, which in its perfection casteth out fear, being entirely extinguished, to it must succeed unchangeable hatred, accompanied with the most tormenting terrours.

But

But in reflecting only that we could draw no confolation from the company in which we fhould then be placed, we have by no means confidered all the evils we fhould fuffer from them. Would the malice of the wicked, think ye, be leffened, by their being rendered defperate? Will the mockeries of the cruel, the taunts of the infolent, the fpite of the revengeful, be reftrained by knowing that their final doom is paft? Or rather, Will not all who are condemned to depart from the throne as curfed, become objects of mutual perfecution to each other, and hell thus be made, even were no external torments added, a fcene of ceafelefs diftrefs, of inexpreffible mifery?

If men could but be perfuaded to apply their thoughts ferioufly to what muft, in the natural courfe of things, be the fufferings of the impenitent in another world, where, even for the fake of the good, they will be entirely feparated from them, and where it would be abfurd to fuppofe, they
will

will be placed in a place purpofely pre-pared to afford eafe to their reftlefs fpirits, they could not but defcry fuch a portion of mifery awaiting obftinate tranfgreffours, in merely being expofed and confined without relief to the company of the damned, as muft make an impreffion on their minds, and convince them, that without adverting to the pofitive penalties denounced by revelation, the future fufferings of thofe who continue in iniquity, will infinitely furpafs all the pleafure they can here gain through the indulgences of fin.

But how then will ftand the accompt, when the pofitive punifhments with which the Gofpel menaces the impenitent, be taken into it? Thefe are, the fire which never goeth out, and the worm which never dieth; and the effects of thefe on the fufferers are defcribed by weeping, and gnafhing of teeth: expreffions which convey to us images of the fevereft torments both of body and mind. While thofe who conceive, they gain an argument againft the

the probability of these, from the presumed impossibility of a material fire, seem to forget, that the wicked, as well as the righteous, shall rise again, with their bodies, to judgement. And after all, however men may amuse themselves with reasoning on the particulars of the future punishment, the power of God will infallibly furnish means to fulfil all that His justice has threatened. As in contemplating, therefore, the everlasting happiness of the good, there appeared no danger of our conceiving too highly of the blessings they will enjoy, so may we be assured, that the fears of the sinner, which prove ineffectual to produce repentance, will never surpass those real sufferings, which he is heaping up for himself against the day of the revelation of the righteous judgement of God.

We may, then, for the purpose of raising in our breasts such an horrour of the penalties of sin, as may deter us from yielding to the temptations of it, without either presumption, or peril of encreasing our apprehensions henfions beyond the reality of the inflictions, picture to ourfelves a vaft abyfs, whofe utter darknefs will be interrupted, not relieved, by the blue glare of fulphurous flames; whofe unmeafured concave will refound with ceafelefs cries of mifery; cries not of a nature to excite compaffion, but to raife horrour. Wherein, if an haplefs wretch would remove from place to place, in hopes of finding fome eafe, inftead of meeting, as in the regions of the bleffed, fmiles of benevolence, and countenances of joy, he will encounter only the fcowl of malice, and the grin of defpair. Where, inftead of the affectionate congratulations of thofe with whom he paft in Chriftian love through this life, he will, on meeting his former affociates in vice, hear only bitter reproaches for the fhare he had in bringing them to that place of torment. For fubjects of meditation he can have only the perverfenefs which brought him into that fcene of mifery, and the fcene itfelf; where the lamentations of the fufferers, without alleviating their own, will

con-

SERM. XI.

contribute to encrease each other's wretchedness; and where, while those who have obtained a contrary lot, receive in the presence of God fulness of joy, they, banished from the light of His countenance, are doomed to dwell with the devil and his angels for ever and ever.

In this course of this address to you, I have repeatedly stated, that the end of calling your attention to these terrours of the Lord, is no other than that of persuading you, if possible, to make timely and effectual exertions for avoiding them. These exertions will necessarily be damped by listening to those vain babblings which would lead you to hope, that they may, in the event, prove less than the Gospel has declared they shall be. The shallowness of such reasonings, therefore, I have endeavoured to expose: and although it be manifest as light itself, that under a wise and just Governour, the disobedient cannot finally be gainers by their transgressions; yet, as multitudes of the sons of Adam are simple

simple enough to overlook this plain truth in their practice, I have reminded you of the declarations of Scripture as to the greatness of the punishments appointed for the impenitent; that by comparing these with whatever enjoyments, ye may imagine, that ye can in this world gain by sin, ye may see how directly contrary to your own everlasting interest ye act, by refusing the narrow path that leadeth to life, and preferring the broad way that endeth in destruction. As, therefore, ye would wish, when all the good ye can obtain in this world shall be at an end, not to be deprived of all prospect of further happiness, not to be cast into outer darkness, there to abide with the devil and his angels in everlasting burnings, surrounded with the cursed, expressing the torments they endure by ceaseless weeping and gnashing of teeth, wisely make an effectual use of what is revealed of these things, and without waiting until one be sent from the dead to testify of their reality, listen, ere your ears are closed by death, to Moses and the prophets, to the Lord Jesus and His apostles, calling you to repentance; and warning you throughout the sacred volume, that there is none other way under Heaven, by which men may avoid the plagues, that are written in that book.

SERMON XII.

ON THE TENDENCY AND USE OF TEMPORAL AFFLICTIONS.

Psalm CXIX. 75.

I know, O Lord, that thy judgements are right, and that Thou in faithfulness hast afflicted me.

AS it is the great end of wisdom to teach us the true road to happiness, one immediate object of its precepts is to instruct us how we may either lessen, or entirely extricate ourselves from the evils which so often attack men in this life: and therefore those in every age who have been esteemed teachers of wisdom, have delivered lessons on this head: how far the

Gentile philosophers have succeeded in those which they have left us, let any who have received benefit from them declare; but to tell a man under affliction that there is little or no evil in the distress he feels is to contradict his senses, while small seems the comfort that can be derived from knowing that others suffer as much as we do, or that our own sufferings might be greater: and when the strongest efforts of human wisdom produce little better consolations than these, intermingled with exhortations to bear our miseries like men, because others have done so, and because though we cannot free ourselves from them, they will sometime or other have an end, the need we have of some higher instructor, who can supply our fainting souls with food more solid, becomes too manifest to be doubted. But where shall we find such a master? The earth, we see, produces none such: it is from Heaven alone that we must look for a physician of our souls.

It is religion, and religion alone, that can inform us how to avoid some of the evils that are so prevalent in the world, how to rescue ourselves from others if seized by them, and even, how under those that are inevitable, to be always rejoicing; and this she can do, by instructing us in the several great truths respecting the providence and attributes of God: for if His providence be universal, if His mercy be over all His works, if nothing unknown to Him can come to pass, and nothing can be done in opposition to His power; then may we be assured, that He knoweth our sufferings; and that the permitting us to continue under them, is consistent with His invariable goodness: and we may estimate the evils which have befallen us as His judgements, which are always right; and be confident, that in very faithfulness He hath caused us to be afflicted. " But how is this (perhaps ye would now ask) your mode of blunting the stings of affliction, telling us we deserve our sufferings? Would you heal our infirmities by wounding our spirits?

rits? Do you strive to lessen our griefs by telling us, the hand of God is upon us? Or, if these things are to be esteemed His judgements, are we to think that all who are in adversity, have brought themselves to it by their sins; and that all the unfortunate are wicked also?" To these questions I will endeavour to reply in their order.

I can then but think, that they reason weakly, and conceive unworthily of the wisdom, power, and goodness of God, who would persuade us, that particular evils are absolutely necessary to the good of the whole, and the sufferings of individuals to the general happiness. Such reasoners appear to me to resemble Job's friends, in presumptuously taking up a cause, with the circumstances of which they are little acquainted, and speaking deceitfully for God. It is true that His providence is perpetually employed in bringing good out of evil, and in remedying those mischiefs which arise from the folly and wickedness of His creatures; But are we therefore to conclude, that

that He originally so formed the world, as to render a partial deformity necessary to the beauty of the whole, and make it impossible that some of its inhabitants should be happy, but at the expence of others? Is his power of communicating happiness so limited, that He can dispense a certain portion only among His creatures? And are the treasures of His goodness so small, that if He would enrich one, He must impoverish another? Let us not entertain imaginations so dishonourable to the great Creatour of the universe, or ascribe to Him a conduct which has so much the appearance of injustice, as the condemning of beings without any demerits of their own to a course of sufferings, merely that they may be subservient to the happiness of others. Let us rather (however mysterious some of the measures of Providence may be, for mysterious many of them must be to creatures short-sighted as we are) rest assured, that whatever any one of us undergoes, tends materially to our own correction or improvement, although it be possible, that others may alfo, at the fame time, be benefited by it: and let us learn to contemplate the providence of God, in that juft, though wonderful light, that while it regulates and governs the univerfe at large, it defcends fo far to the private concerns of the meaneft individual, that even the hairs of our heads are all numbered; and confider His wifdom and power to be fuch, that even the variety and complication of men's temporal interefts can raife no impediment to His dealing by every one of us with the moft exact juftice, and abundant mercy. This will be thinking of the Lord our God as we ought to think; it will be holding with the well-inftructed and truly religious in all ages: and if we thus entertain the fame fentiment with them, we fhall experience the fame confolation from it which they received. For fuppofe ye that when the pfalmift was able to make the reflection contained in the text, his anguifh was encreafed by it? No; though on the firft attack of adverfity, when he faw the ftorm gathering on all fides, the

con-

confcioufnefs of his fins augmented his terrours, and made his forrow ftill more bitter, fo as to force him to exclaim, "A wounded fpirit who can bear!" When he grew fufficiently collected in mind to confider the character of the Judge under whofe fentence he was fuffering, and that his heavenly Father ever feafoned juftice with mercy, the horrours of his foul were calmed, he viewed his prefent ills as probable fources of the higheft good, and acknowledged the kindnefs of God in thus correcting him, by faying, "It is good for me that I have been afflicted, that I may learn thy ftatutes."

And fuch is the natural and happy confequence of a juft idea and firm belief of the univerfality of the divine providence. For evils, with the fource of which we are unacquainted, affect us the more feverely, becaufe being at a lofs for their origin, we are unable, too, to conjecture when they will end: but when fatisfied that they fall to our lot, under the direction of God's wifdom and mercy, we have this comfortable

able assurance, that they are intended either for our correction, in which case they will be withdrawn, whenever that is brought about, an event that we have it in our own power to accelerate, by amending what, on an examination of our conduct, we find amiss therein, or for our improvement by trial, that we may attain an everlasting inheritance among those who are made perfect through sufferings; and therefore from whichever cause they proceed, it is ours to search the matter to the bottom, convinced that we are neither unreasonably nor unjustly subjected to affliction: while by the same mode of reasoning we may preserve ourselves from putting any uncharitable interpretations on the cases of others, and from conceiving that they are worse than other men whose misfortunes are more severe; since " whom the Lord loveth He chasteneth, and scourgeth every son whom He receiveth." Neither, I presume, is there any good reason to think, that a common case, which is related in the Gospel, of the man who was born blind, that the glory of of God might be shewed forth on him, by our Lord's imparting sight unto him. Indeed, if we fairly consider the circumstances of it, he cannot be said to have suffered any evil, since, having never experienced the blessings of light, the want of it could but little affect him.

Amply, indeed, doth holy scripture set forth to us, through various passages, that cultivation with which our merciful Creatour favours, and by which, but for our own stubborn and perverse resistance, He would perfect the sons of men. "Foolish men (saith the psalmist) are plagued for their offence, and because of their wickedness:" and the prophets frequently represent to us, under the image of an husbandman's management of his vineyard, or his field, God's dispensations for the correction of that people, whose history hath been preserved for the instruction of all succeeding ages: and our blessed Lord hath likened Himself to a vine, and his disciples to the branches of it, declaring, that every branch
which

SERM. XII.

which beareth not fruit, His Father will take away; but thofe which do bear fruit, He will purge, that they may bring forth more fruit. Hence, then, we may learn to put a juft conftruction on whatever temporal evils may befal us; and as on the one hand, we may be affured, that fince God is not unjuft, He will not needlefsly fubject us to mifery; fo on the other, we fhould reflect, that if we want correction, He muft ceafe to be merciful, before He can fail to give it us.

Neither is it enormous wickednefs only, or a confirmed habit of vice, that requires the remedy of punifhment; the application of the fame medicine on our very firft tranfgreffions may, in truth, be an act of mercy, and prevent evil difpofitions from taking fo deep root in our breafts as to render a long courfe of fufferings neceffary to eradicate them; nay, further, as a wife phyfician would ever prefer a preventive to a remedy, it may be fit, that even the innocent fhould meet with croffes, and fuch afflictions as may

may preclude them from opportunities of falling into bad habits, and from temptations to sin; against which, though they are not aware of them, their heavenly Father thus mercifully guards them. Dangerous is the security that arises from prosperity; many and rank are the weeds that spring from so rich a soil; ought we then to complain of the hand that keeps our souls from such? or should we not rather bless Him, who thus preserves us from perils, against which, from our ignorance, we cannot even ask for His assistance? "The heart is deceitful above all things," saith the prophet; and if this be the case, how often may there be lurking in our breasts evil principles, which, though we ourselves be not conscious of it, require the correction of adversity? Even many of those things which, were the judgement of the world asked, it would determine to be but foibles, might prove, if suffered to continue in our breast, impediments to our enjoyment of perfect happiness in whatever state we were.

SERM. XII.

Ye see then to how many causes, in which we ourselves only are concerned, the afflictions we undergo may be ascribed; and how great reason we have, under all our sorrows, to address ourselves to God, in confidence that they are His judgements which are right, and to confess that in faithfulness He hath afflicted us. There are several evils which we see attached to particular courses of vice as their natural punishment; and that all others are sent either for the correction or prevention of sins, or the trial and confirmation of virtue, there is every ground to believe, since the nature and state of man, the attributes of God, and the declarations of Scripture, all tend to justify this belief. And if such be our faith, what should in wisdom be our practice? If we know, that to conquer the stubborn heart, it must be bowed down by sorrows; that correction is necessary to the rooting out of evil dispositions, and that crosses and disappointment are requisite to the destruction of vicious habits, we cannot be insensible that it is highly absurd to enter

on

on such courses from which we cannot return but through affliction, and our following which calls for punishment as an effect of the very mercy of God. While, on the other hand, the same considerations will tend to preserve us from despondency under sufferings, and to keep alive in us that hope and trust, which are the best incitements to resolute and effectual exertions. If we be convinced, that the ills which overtake us are not the decrees of an irresistible fate, or the effects of blind chance, but those judgements which an all-wise and good God inflicts, and adapts to the circumstances of our case, this lesson will present itself unto us; that it is ours to forward, as much as in us lies, His gracious purposes, and to hasten, by every mean in our power, that amendment or improvement, towards which His dispensations are thus directed, and at the same time that we shall receive no small satisfaction in the thought, that our Creatour is working together with us for our deliverance from errour, and our obtainment of salvation, we cannot fail to perceive,

ceive, that if, purfuing a contrary courfe, we give no heed to the more early warnings He vouchfafes us, but harden ourfelves againft his chaftifements, and will not fee the hand that is ftretched out over us, either our afflictions muft be increafed until we do feel, or a fentence of final condemnation be pronounced againft us, as defperate and incorrigible finners.

Thus doth our all-perfect Governour and Judge fet life and death before us, not only repeatedly calling on us to make, but, if we be going wrong, admonifhing us to correct our choice; every rejection of fuch warning will naturally and juftly render our return to the right way more difficult, though we may not be totally deprived of the power of undertaking it until life itfelf clofes: then, indeed, the time of probation being paft, when the finner finds the folly of his choice, and looks back on the opportunities he hath miffed, the warnings he hath rejected, and the mercies he hath defpifed, his fhame, remorfe, and anguifh, muft must be what no powers of language can express. Imagine a soul freed from the deceptions by which the world blinds us, sensible that all the good it can receive during the whole of its existence, is already past, conscious of the happiness of that state from which its own perverseness alone hath excluded it, and feeling the misery to which, by the just sentence of God, it is for ever condemned; and when ye have considered the bitter agonies such a soul must endure, reflect, that if ye begin not to-day, while it is called to-day, to work out your salvation, these agonies must be your own, since the night cometh, when no man can work.

On the other hand, to encourage us steadily to go through the labour of recovering that ground which we may have lost in the race that is set before us, let us further think on the bliss enjoyed by those who, through the assistance afforded them by their almighty Patron, have come off conquerors in their spiritual warfare; what ecstasy must such feel, when in the presence of Him who hath redeemed them out of every kindred, and tongue, and people, and nation, they reflect on the dangers from which they have been delivered; and comparing the miseries they have escaped with the happiness they now taste, with hearts overflowing with gratitude, cast the crowns of glory which they have received before the throne, and with ceaseless alleluias ascribe unto Him who sitteth thereon, and unto the Lamb, blessing and glory, and wisdom and thanksgiving, and honour and power.

SERMON XIII.

ON THE SPRING.

PSALM CIV. 14.

He causeth the grass to grow for the cattle, and herb for the service of man; that he may bring forth food out of the earth.

THE psalm whence these words are selected, is particularly well known; its being wholly taken up in the mention of those works of God which are visible to every eye, and the grateful strain which pervades it, for the wonders which He hath wrought, and the bountiful provision He hath prepared for all the creatures which exist on earth, and more especially for man, into whose hands the rest are given, seem to have recommended it to general notice. *Who, indeed, can* be infenfible to the juftice of thofe praifes which the pfalmift here offers to his Creatour? or not partake in thofe fenfations which he, with fuch unaffected earneftnefs expreffes, on contemplating the admirable proofs of divine goodnefs, wifdom, and power, which every part of the world prefents unto us? There is need of neither the acquirements of learning, nor the endowments of philofophy, to render our minds fufceptible of fuch impreffions from the various teftimonies of the unfpeakable glory of the Lord, exhibited to us in the moft common operations of His providence, as will excite us to join in lauding and magnifying *His* name, of whofe riches the earth is full, and whofe mercy is over all his works. Our advancement in knowledge will conftantly fupply us with additional reafon, every new difcovery yield further ground for wonder, love and praife; and the more extenfive our enquiries are, the more accurate our refearches, the richer will become the fcene of divine beneficence

beneficence displayed to our view. Still even those who, by their situation in life, have been debarred from the more ample means of instruction, and whose natural faculties have received no further improvement than what is derived from common intercourse with the world, cannot be blind to those splendid proofs of their Maker's power and munificence that present themselves in the manner in which this globe is fitted for the accommodation of the various tribes of animals that dwell on it, or deaf to the calls for gratitude thence arising on themselves.

The benefits accruing to the inhabitants of the earth, from the nature and situation of the heavenly bodies, from the heat of the sun, and from the light and influence of the moon, from the clouds raised by the former to fall again in fruitful and refreshing showers, from the tides occasioned by the last; the grateful vicissitude of day and night, by which seasons adapted to our necessary labours and the rest required, alter-

alternately succeed each other, the usefulness of the numberless rivers with which the earth is watered, and of the metals and different substances with which its mountains and its bowels abound; and various ways in which all the living things we see thereon, contribute to each other's support, are discernible by every eye, and may be comprehended by every understanding: while the blessings which they afford by being general, demand acknowledgement and thanksgiving from every individual. In the attempt, therefore, which I shall now make to call your minds to the consideration of that beauteous portion of the wonderful works of the Lord, which does at this season of the year begin to shine with peculiar lustre, I trust, I shall meet with universal attention.

The vegetable world is now coming into its most florid state: every plant from the towering oak to the humblest herbs, now bursts forth in new luxuriance; and whether we view them separately or collectively, they

they afford both by their beauty, and the manner in which they administer to the support and comfort of our lives, matter of reflection so obvious, and so capable of furnishing both pleasure and improvement, that to be surrounded with them as we are, and receive as we do, hourly satisfaction therefrom, yet notice not the sources of it, would betray a degree of insensibility disgraceful to any one who claims the name of man. Behold the earth clothed with verdure, and abundantly pouring forth her various productions; see the grass growing for the cattle, and herb for the service of man: mark the trees of the forest how strongly they shoot, and the fruit trees putting forth their innumerable blossoms; how the meads are bedecked with flowers, and the fields stand thick with corn! Then consider this great thing; that all these plants differing among themselves in numberless degrees with respect to growth, colour, shape and property, do yet all spring from the same ground, are nourished by the same showers, and warmed by the same sun.

sun. The slender cypress, and the huge cedar, will flourish in the same plantation; the quick-growing lofty elm, and the tardy humble yew, grow side by side; and the same bed displays the bright yellow of the crocus, the deep blue of the violet, the lilly's unsullied white, and all the tints of the gaudy tulip. Are there found, then, in the earth, peculiar particles already prepared and severally adapted to the production of each of these, and are their roots so formed as to select those only which belong to their own plant? and does the diversity arise from thence? Or, is the whole texture of the plant originally contained in the seed, and gradually unfolding and enlarging itself as supplied from the soil with food, does it, by a process of natural chymistry, purify the matter conveyed to it by its root, and throwing off all that is superfluous and unfit, retain and dispense to its several parts that alone which is adequate to give unto each its proper substance, size and colour? Now, were the former the case, the graff of one kind inserted into the

the stock of another, would, if it bore at all, bear the fruit of the stock, in lieu of that of its parent tree; while the structure of plants, and the uses of their several parts, justify the opinion, that the last, though no less miraculous, is the true account of their growth. For that nutriment which the root evidently draws from the earth, must be strained through the greater vessels of the stem, before it can enter the leaves; where again running through those veins which are visible to the naked eye, it is fitted for the channels of the finer shoots, and of those leaves which cover the flower; but it is not until it has been through the flower itself that it becomes of sufficient purity to enter those vessels wherein the seed of the plant is generated. It is, then, by the changes which the sap undergoes in the plant itself, that it is enabled gradually to fill out its various parts, and contribute to the manifestation of its peculiar beauties: and stupendous as is the thought, there must be contained, in the small compass of an acorn, the original texture of the trunk,

and

and all the numerous branches into which the spreading oak gradually expands itself.

Nor will the manner in which the several elements contribute to forward this growth, the assistance it receives from the frequent returns of day and night, and even from the more turbulent agitations of the air, and the care with which the shoot of the following spring is in the bud, defended against the severity of winter, fail to reward our attention to them, by discovering to us such traces of divine wisdom and power, as will raise in our minds affections that will tend to make us both happier and better. And if from the structure and growth of plants in general, we pass on to consider, how calculated the several species are to supply the various wants of the animal world, our admiration and our gratitude will meet with calls equally awakening.

It did not escape the holy psalmist's notice, that the goodness of Providence extendeth even to the fowls of the air, in pro-

providing an habitation meet for them. He speaks of the cedars of Lebanon, which the Lord hath planted, where the birds make their nests. As for the stork, says he, the fir-trees are her house: And shall we overlook the more striking instances of the divine bounty? Shall we forget with what variety of timber adapted to such different uses, He furnishes us by the trees of the forest; the abundance of herbs and fruits, He causeth our gardens to yield; the provender He gives us for the support of our cattle, or the grain for our own subsistence? Living in the midst of these, and being accustomed to behold their production, we perceive no miracle therein. But if reflect on the one hand, how requisite they are to our comfort, and even to our existence; and on the other, that we brought them not into the world with us, but found them ready provided for our accommodation; and that even towards their encrease or continuance, our power goeth not far, since one man planteth and another watereth, but God giveth the encrease; we shall discern,

discern, that it is with the fruit of His works that the earth is satisfied; and if we carry our observation a little further, discover that in wisdom He hath ordained them all. For those plants which are the most wanted, and are of the most extensive use, are of the most usual growth, and easiest cultivation; and the products of each climate are the best suited to the necessities of its inhabitants. For the raising of our corn, we want not the shelter of walls, nor the borrowed warmth of glasses; the common labour of the husbandman is sufficient: and were less than this required, were men not obliged to labour that they may gain what is necessary to a comfortable subsistence, the idleness reigning among them would soon make the world present one scene of uncurbed licentiousness, even more abominable than that which is exhibited by some of the affluent in the present day. But if not content with the common fruits of their country, men seek to enjoy those which other climates boast; in the cultivation of these, more labour is required, and happily

happily so, since such wishes are not raised among the people until they are got into that state of society, and their numbers are so encreased, that many want employment, and additional occupations are necessary to furnish business for the additional hands. And yet further, while to those animals whose assistance man needeth in his labours, the wilderness and the desart yield but scanty provision, to the wilder kinds they, throughout the year, afford more ample subsistence. Thus wisely are the products of the ground apportioned! Thus all wait upon the Lord, and He giveth them their meat in due season: He giveth to the beast his food, and feedeth the young ravens which cry; He giveth them, they gather; He openeth His hand, they are filled with good.

Neither are His gifts confined to what is necessary; magnificent in ornament, and ample are His works, affording many gratifications innocent and elegant: the never-satiating green which the leaves display,

the

SERM. XIII.

the various hues which both the bloſſoms and fruits preſent to the eye, and the different ſcents with which the ſmell is regaled by the plants, afford pleaſures which we may enjoy without ſin, and in which we may indulge without impurity.

Having thus recommended to your contemplation that ſcene of divine wiſdom, power, and munificence, which does now in particular claim our attention, let me further ſuggeſt to you ſome improvements which the ſacred writers notice as naturally ariſing from a review of theſe things.

At the cloſe of the hymn whence the text is taken, we find the pſalmiſt expreſſing, in the following ſtrain, his thankfulneſs to God, for all the mighty works he had been contemplating: " I will ſing unto the Lord as long as I live; I will ſing praiſe unto my God while I have my being; my meditation of Him ſhall be ſweet; I will be glad in the Lord!" and concluding with

with an exhortation to others to render likewife their praifes, " Praife ye the Lord." And verily, fuch is the call for thankfgiving hereby made on us, that we muſt be convinced of the moſt ſtupid ingratitude, if we fail to render it; ſince thefe mercies are not at a diſtance that we cannot defcry them, neither are they trifling, that we may overlook them, but we feel them in our raiment, we taſte them in our food, and we meet them in all our ways. Oh, that men would therefore praife the Lord for His goodnefs, and for His wonderful works to the children of men! That they would not, with thanklefs inattention receive, but with grateful hearts *rejoice*, in His bounty; and while they live on His benevolence, accept likewife the inſtruction He fets before them in His mode of imparting it!

" I went by the field of the flothful," fays the wife man, " and by the vineyard of the man void of underſtanding, and Lo! it was all grown over with thorns, and nettles had covered the face thereof:" And what

what was the leſſon he drew therefrom? Even this; "Yet a little ſleep, a little ſlumber, a little folding of the hands to ſleep, ſo ſhall thy poverty come as one that travelleth, and thy want as an armed man." See then Nature ſo conſtituted by her great Creatour as to yield her fruit only at Labour's earneſt call; thorns and thiſtles form the crop of the ſlothful; but the diligent ſhe plenteouſly rewardeth. See the well-cultivated field, how it flouriſheth, and that he who keepeth his fig-tree, eateth the fruit thereof; and hence learn, that idleneſs was not made for man, nor ſhall the ſluggard be ſatisfied with encreaſe.

Again; "Conſider the lilies of the field how they grow; they toil not, neither do they ſpin: And yet I ſay unto you, that even Solomon in all his glory was not arrayed like one of theſe. Wherefore, if God ſo clothe the graſs of the field which to-day is, and to-morrow is caſt into the oven, Shall He not much more cloath you, O ye of little faith!" Such were the words of of our blessed Lord to His disciples; and such is the comfort we are taught to gather when menaced with penury, and fearful of distress, from that scene of divine power and munificence which even this portion of the creation displayeth! The glories with which the flowers of the field are decked, evidently leave, at an immeasurable distance, all the ornaments which human art can furnish; it is plain, too, that they are *not of their own* providing, but received from their Creatour's hand: And if His providence so richly extends to creatures thus mean in comparison with man, Shall it not much more extend to man himself? Or shall aught prevent our partaking of the blessings of His bounty, but our own ill behaviour? That indeed may, and many and fearful have been the instances of this exhibited in the world. It is not always that the labours of man prosper; the best course of tillage will not alone ensure a plentiful crop; favourable seasons are necessary to crown it with success; and these are withholden when the Lord in His justice sees fit, to make a fruitful land barren, for the wickedness of those that dwell therein.

But there is yet another lesson resulting from the subject before us; a lesson humiliating indeed, but salutary, and well adapted to correct the fervour with which we embrace the things of this life, and that forgetfulness which we so frequently betray of the uncertainty of our continuance in it. How often does it happen, that the flower whose beauties we admire in the morning, fadeth ere the day closes! its colours gone, its odours past, it hangs its drooping head, and only testifies, by its sad remains, the rapidity of its decay; And is the glory of man more durable? Are not his days as grafs? He flourisheth in the morning, but is fallen off and withered at night: Alas! some of us may never *reach* the evening of life! What numbers blasted by chilling winds, or parched by the mid-day's sun, suddenly disappear, and their place knoweth them no more! And how soon may the most florid among us come into that state, in which it shall justly be pronounced over him, " Man that is born of a woman hath but a short time to live, and is full of misery: he cometh up, and is cut down like a flower: he fleeth as it were a shadow, and never continueth in one stay!"

But, blessed be God! the parallel endeth not here. Those beauties which every tree, and every herb, now discloseth, have succeeded to the ravage of winter: in the year past they exhibited the like beauties, but gradually decaying as the unfavourable rigour of the season encreased, their vegetative powers became at length dormant and inactive; inactive, but not destroyed; concealed, but not lost. Behold them rising from the tomb of winter, and bursting forth with all the vigour of renewed life! And shall not this bring to our minds the wonderful fact which was by the power of the Lord brought about in the person of our blessed Saviour? Behold a man seemingly stricken of God, vexed with all His storms, and cut off from the land of the living, then laid for a season in the darkness of the sepulchre, but quickly breaking from the bands of death, and so unexpectedly appearing to his followers, that while they yet know Him not, they with sorrowful hearts complain unto Himself, that they had trusted, that it had been He who would have redeemed Israel. Mark the grain, which awhile ago was buried in the earth, now springing up with a new body, and ye will then see the absurdity of starting speculative difficulties against the doctrine of a resurrection, and the folly of putting the questions, How are the dead raised up, or with what body do they come? Behold, to every seed God giveth its own body; and that He will do so likewise to every man, He hath given us assurance, in that He hath raised up Christ as the first fruits from the grave; promising, that to those who have true faith in Him, and who are, indeed, His disciples, the valley of the shadow of death, shall prove a passage to the mount of God, to the heavenly Jerusalem, and to an innumerable company of angels,

angels, to the general assembly and church of the first-born, which are written in Heaven, and to God the Judge of all, and to the spirits of just men made perfect, and to Jesus the Mediatour of the new covenant.

These are the improvements which the contemplation of the beautiful scene the earth now presents, naturally suggests to us; let not then the season pass without accepting them; learn to admire and adore the all-glorious perfections of the Creatour; sleep not over his bounty, but industriously employ the powers, and cultivate the means of happiness He hath given you, firmly trust in his exuberant goodness, dread his power, and stand in awe of His justice: be mindful of the frailty of your own existence; and remember, that uncertain as it is in its present state, and dark as appears the hour which closes it, the infinite mercy of God does, through the mediation of His Son, now offer you opportunity, an opportunity, if once lost, never to be recovered, of securing to yourselves a better life, and exchanging the terrours of death, and the night of the grave, for the joys of a triumphant refurrection, and the ever blooming happinefs of His eternal day.

SERMON XIV.

ON THE HARVEST.

GEN. VIII. 22.

While the earth remaineth, seed time and harvest, cold and heat, summer and winter, and day and night, shall not cease.

THESE words, in which the sacred historian has recorded the divine purpose never more while this world itself shall endure, to interrupt the stated succession of the seasons, and of the alternate periods for labour and for rest given unto men, will furnish Christians with an answer to the question ascribed by St. Peter to the scoffers of the last days, " Where is the promise of His coming? for since the fathers

fathers fell asleep, all things continue as they were from the beginning of the creation." For if it has been declared by revelation, that the courſe of the material world ſhould ſuffer no conſiderable interruption, its having yet ſuffered none ſuch, yields teſtimony in favour of revelation; and, conſequently, of the truth of that promiſe, which the wicked naturally wiſh may never be fulfilled, that the Lord will return to render to every man according to his works. Nay, further, ſince in the following words of ſcripture, " Thus ſaith the Lord: If ye can break my covenant of the day, and my covenant of the night, and that there ſhould not be day and night in their ſeaſon, then may alſo my covenant be broken with David my ſervant, that he ſhould not have a ſon to reign upon his throne; and with the Levites the prieſts, my miniſters," the ſtability of the former covenant is pointed out as a pledge of that of the other, with the full completion of which, our bleſſed Saviour's ſecond coming is ſo neceſſarily connected, the uninterrupted performance of of it forms, under thefe circumftances, no lefs than a perpetual admonition, that He whofe word fupports the one, will, in His own good time, fulfil the other alfo.

Of the firft, as far as it involves in it a promife that the world fhall never more be deftroyed by water, He hath inftituted a fign: " And God faid, This is the token of the covenant which I make between Me and you, and every living creature that is with you, for perpetual generations: I do fet my bow in the cloud; and it fhall be for a token of a covenant between Me and the earth." Hence even among the Heathen, when they had forgotten the real occafion of this token being appointed, the rainbow was ftill confidered as a fign from Heaven; and was perfonified by the poets under the character of a Meffenger between their feigned gods and men. But fhould that appearance which, although from the defect of their information it caufed them to entertain fuperftitious opinions, and to run into idolatrous practices, plainly made

a deep

a deep religious impreſſion on their minds, be ſo frequently ſeen by us, who are acquainted with the everlaſting covenant of which it has been appointed the ſign, without recalling to our remembrance that hand, by which the whole ſyſtem of Heaven and earth is ſupported? Or ſhould we ſuffer the ſeveral ſeaſons continually to revolve in their regular ſucceſſion, without devoutly acknowledging, how much we owe to God for cauſing ſeed time and harveſt, and cold and heat, and ſummer and winter, and day and night, ceaſeleſsly to ſucceed each other?

That we may be guiltleſs of an omiſſion ſo ungrateful at the preſent ſeaſon, which ſeems particularly to call for our praiſe and thankſgiving, becauſe it is that which crowns the reſt, by bringing into our garners thoſe fruits of the earth, to the production of which all the other ſeaſons in their turns contributed, I have ſelected the words of the text for the ſubject of my preſent addreſs to you; purpoſing to make uſe of the opportunity which they afford me, of remind-

reminding you how necessary the several periods mentioned in the words before us are for carrying on the great work of vegetation, and conducting the plants, by which the animal world is supported, through the various stages of their growth, from the first appearance of the blade, to the time when they are ripe for the harvest; and thence to proceed to state to you some practical inferences, which naturally arise from a review of this portion of the divine wisdom and goodness towards us.

I may justly, I think, suppose, that there is no man who, when he either casts his eye upon the fields before the sickle is put to them, or sees the reapers scattered over the land, or observes the wains groaning under the loads which they are bearing to the barn, does not feel his soul affected with a sense of the bounty of that hand which thus scatters plenty over the earth, and of the greatness of Him, Who hath so framed it, that it is thus abundant in its productions. But to those who are not un-
accustomed

SERM. accustomed to contemplate their Creatour's
XIV. works as such, and meditate on the traces of infinite wisdom and goodness discernible therein, these objects, as opening a still wider field for observation and praise, yield much greater delight. Yet the full satisfaction to be received from them cannot be enjoyed even by such, unless they take into consideration various circumstances which are wonderfully combined for forwarding and conducting to its due perfection every plant the earth produces. Our present review must be principally confined to what the several seasons contribute to these ends.

Of the seasons, then, that which may, to a superficial observer, appear adverse, is, in reality, friendly to vegetation, the very winter itself performing a part of essential importance towards the plenty of the ensuing seasons. Vegetables draw merely from the earth itself much less of that which supports and enlarges them, than is, probably, by most men imagined. The chief part of their nutriment is conveyed by by water: and the air contributes much to their preservation. Now of the former of these elements, the winter yields the great supply by its rains and snow; while by its winds and frosts it purifies the latter. Necessary is that abundance of the first which then descends upon our lands; both as to its quantity, being the principal portion of the stock from whence the encrease of the future year is to be supplied; and as to its quality, it having acquired by the natural process it has gone through, of exhalation from the earth, and of impregnation in the air, all the softness and penetrating powers which render it capable of promoting their growth, and rendering the plants prolifick. And without the winds and frost, vegetable as well as animal life would suffer much from that impurity of the air which these contribute to remove. While the latter of them penetrating into the ground does, when on the approach of spring it is resolved, break its clods, and prepare it for the reception of seeds, and render it easy to be penetrated by the first tender fibres which

the

the roots put forth: and the former quickly drying from the branches of the trees, the superabundance of that moisture (which, though necessary to the land, if suffered to remain on them, would render them diseased, and cause the bud in which the shoot is wrapped, to rot) prevent great and wide-extending damage.

The soil being thus prepared by winter, the seed time next succeeds, mild in its temperature, neither impeding vegetation by intense cold, nor scorching the infant plants by the excess of its heat; bringing with it frequent showers to water the newly-sown land, and gales, which shaking the plants, not only loosen the earth about their roots, thus forwarding their growth, but agitating so strongly the trunks, branches, and leaves, promote a freer circulation of the sap contained in them; and thus throw off whatever being unremoved might diminish their vigour, and obstruct their growth. The luxuriance of this period affords a covering to the ground against the heat of the

the enfuing feafon, and intercepting, by innumerable leaves, the rays of the fun, caufe their power to be fpent on thofe parts where it is moft neceffary, while the roots kept cool are able to perform their function, and fupply additional nourifhment, until the fruit arrived at its due fize no longer needs fuch.

To bring this to pafs, however, fummer funs are neceffary, by which the juice of the plants undergoes, as it were, an higher diftillation, whereby is produced that fine flour with which the feed veffels are firft filled, and which, by the continuance of the heat drying away the leaves that cover them, is afterwards confolidated into a body, and forms the feed itfelf: and which feed, if not gathered now by man, having by the fame means that coat which contains it dried until it burfts, falls to the ground for the fupply of plants for the enfuing year. Thus wonderfully is the fucceffion of feafons conftituted to bring the fruits of the earth to that perfection in which they are gathered,

gathered, and made the support of animal life. In warmer climes, indeed, the annual revolution proceeds not through the same periods; but that purification of the air of which their inhabitants would otherwise be deprived through want of the winter's frosts, is for them provided by means of more violent rains, of lightning, and of hurricanes. While the products of their lands require greater heat to bring them to maturity; and without such fruits, wisely and mercifully suited to their climes, they would soon perish from countries on which the sun directly darteth down his rays.

Neither should we pass, without observation, the utility of the shorter periods of day and night, and their mutual succession to the same important end, the growth of every plant. Those vessels which the heat of the sun had, during the day, caused to expand, and not only supplied with sap from the root, but opened their numerous pores to receive the dews which fall on his descent, being, by the coldness of the night, rapidly

rapidly compreffed, thereby force the juices with which they are filled every way, and make the buds to fhoot. And hence it is that all vegetables grow more by night than day; except, perhaps, during fhowers, when the rain fills the pores, and its coldnefs does the office of the night air.

Thus have all the various viciffitudes to which our atmofphere is fubject to their ufe, and thus neceffary to all who dwell on the earth, is the conftant continuance of the divine determination mentioned in the text, " While the earth remaineth, feed time and harveft, and cold and heat, and fummer and winter, and day and night, fhall not ceafe." Is it not ours, therefore, by reflecting on what God herein doth for man, to ftrive to learn what it becomes us, under the receipt of thefe continued mercies, on our part to do?

Behold then, firft, the call and encouragement here holden forth to unwearied diligence in our labour: fince in every ftep we take,

take, God is working with us, amply rewarding all our pains by the fertility to which His seasons give birth, and yet having so constituted the earth, that in proportion as man ceases to exert himself, his supply of food decreases. This lesson, as shewing how greatly an idle life differs from that which our Maker would, that we should lead, merits both the most serious attention of individuals, who very frequently seem to think, that they are at liberty to spend, or rather to waste their time in sloth, or what is next to sloth, the most trifling amusements, provided they injure not others; as if He who, in the material world, hath made nothing but to a good end, had yet endowed man, the creature to whom He has put so many others into subjection, with all his wondrous powers of actions for none; and the consideration of communities, which sometimes overlook that which, if duely attended to, would preserve in them a measure of good order, integrity, and happiness, which, I much fear, has by this inattention, departed from our own country

never

never to return; that God hath, in His natural world, taught the same thing which His apostle Paul delivers in the form of a precept: " For even when we were with you, this we commanded you, that if any would not work, neither should he eat."

Another point, suggested by the review we have taken, is that of our utter dependence on the goodness of God. Unless He were mindful of His covenant for ever, and of His promise from generation to generation, the Heavens over our head might be as brass, and the earth under us as iron: we might carry out much seed into the field, and bring but little in: we might plant vineyards and dress them, but neither drink of the wine, nor gather the grapes from them. Reflections of this kind are too seldom made, and too little encouraged among men. Content with knowing the more immediate causes by which they are supplied with food and raiment, they look no farther, but, in the language of holy writ, sacrifice unto their net, and burn incense unto their drag. Yet this our dependance is not such that the recollection of it need either hurt our pride, or lessen our security. To be the objects of a monarch's favour, is flattering to the mind; to have the support of sovereign power, naturally raises confidence. When the blessings we enjoy, flow from the benevolence of the King eternal, almighty, invisible, the only wise God; when it is by the word of the Father of all mercies, with Whom there is no variableness, or shadow of turning, that we live; as our obligations encrease in proportion to the greatness and constancy of our benefactor. For what other sensation is there in this case room, than that of the sincerest gratitude? of gratitude, leading us not to conceal, but to proclaim how greatly we are indebted to Him: not, indeed, by ostentation in our religious acts, but by an unremitted attention to His laws, by readily joining in those publick acknowledgements which His church renders, especially those of the sabbath, (His own appointment of which makes the neglect of it it an act of positive disobedience, of real revolt from His authority) and by teaching our households, and our children after us, to love and to fear Him, as their Maker, their Preserver, and their Judge.

Neither do the improvements of the subject before us stop here. By reflecting on the never-ceasing bounty of Heaven to ourselves, there is an hope that our hearts may be softened into benevolence towards our brethren: from the measure with which it has been meted unto us, we may learn to measure unto others, and be ever after our power ready to give, glad to distribute; and from observing how our heavenly Father maketh His sun to rise on the evil, and on the good, and sendeth rain on the just, and on the unjust; giving even to men who walk in their own ways fruitful seasons, filling their hearts with food and gladness, we may discern the superior glory of loving our enemies, blessing them that curse us, doing good to them that hate us, and praying for them which despitefully use us, we may become the children of our Father which is in Heaven.

But yet, further, if God hath made such bountiful provision for the sons of men as to external goods, Can it be believed, that He would leave the race abandoned in other respects, and not furnish them with what is no less important to their happiness, instruction in the truth, the food of the mind? Yet, if our Gospel come not from Him, this He must have done; Or, if the effects of His benevolence be so great in this transient and uncertain state, How gloriously must they shine forth in the everlasting kingdom prepared for those who love Him? Reasoning after this manner from what our merciful Creatour has done for us as to our natural, to what He will do for us as to our spiritual state, from the comforts with which He supplieth us during our short stay here, to what we may hope for in those mansions where we are to abide for ever, is making a wise and the proper use of the objects now before us, rendering them not snares

to

to entrap our affections, and attach us to what we cannot keep, but subjects of encouragement to press forward to the high prize of our calling. Nor to this end are there wanting, in the holy scriptures, suggestions of a similarity between man in his temporal state, and the vegetables which he cultivates for his support. Like them, he is termed a plant; like them, he is described as flourishing by the protection of the Almighty, and as withering when that is withdrawn: and, like them, (an observation especially adapted to the present season) as having, when ripe for the harvest, the sickle put unto him, and, if good, being gathered like wheat into the garner of the master, and, if bad, like weeds burnt with unquenchable fire. Let us therefore, when we look on the fields that are reaped, recollect, that the period is approaching in which the world will be the same; and the things which now remain according to promise, will, according to promise, likewise be done away; and the following words of Him that sitteth on the throne be fulfilled, " Behold, I make all things new!"

SERMON XV.

ON THE SIGNS OF TIMES.

REV. III. 19.

As many as I love, I rebuke and chasten: be zealous, therefore, and repent.

THE epistles to the seven churches of Asia, contained in this and the foregoing chapter, have, by interpreters of great name, been supposed not to relate solely to the state of those churches at the time when St. John was commanded to send them, but to contain, likewise, a prophetick outline of the state of the whole church in general during seven distinct periods, which were to succeed each other between the time of the apostle's receiving the revelation and that of of our blessed Saviour's coming again: and this supposition is confirmed first, by the proclamation repeated at the end of each epistle, "He that hath an ear, let him hear what the spirit saith unto the churches," so similar to the charge with which our Lord's discourse to His apostles on the signs of His coming again, as recorded by St. Mark, is closed, "And what I say unto you, I say unto all, Watch:" and, secondly, by the state of the church in these several periods having actually corresponded with the description of it contained in the epistles.

But if this be so, it will be natural to ask, Where is the period during which we ourselves live described? In the epistle it may be answered, to the church of the Laodiceans, which is the last of the seven, and from which I have taken the words of my text, so justly descriptive of the cause of the afflictions now poured on Christendom, and of the only means by which we can render our prayers for their removal acceptable:

acceptable: "As many as I love, I rebuke and chasten: be zealous, therefore, and repent."

The cause, ye see, here assigned for the chastening of the Lord, is His love towards us; which moves Him to try all means to bring us to repentance, that we may not be condemned with the world; and since these chastisements consequently cannot be removed, until they have affected the counsels of His mercy, or we are become obdurate, and the objects of final judgements, the only means by which we can secure the acceptance of our petitions for the removal of them, must be those of sincere repentance and real amendment.

But there is, in the words before us too, a suggestion, that we do in one particular more especially stand in need of such amendment, that of religious zeal and heartfelt attachment to the cause of God and His Christ: "Be zealous, therefore." And whether the character given of the Laodiceans

ceans in this respect be as I have asserted, applicable to the present generation of Christians, and to us of this land among the rest, ye may judge, from the particulars of the epistle which I will now state to you, compared with those points of our own conduct, which I shall also call to your remembrance.

" I know thy works, (said our Lord to this type of ourselves) that thou art neither cold nor hot: I would thou wert cold or hot. So then because thou art lukewarm, and neither cold nor hot, I will spew thee out of my mouth. Because thou sayest, I am rich, and encreased with goods, and have need of nothing; and knowest not that thou art wretched, and miserable, and poor, and blind and naked; I counsel thee to buy of me gold tried in the fire, that thou mayest be rich; and white raiment that thou mayest be clothed, and that the shame of thy nakedness do not appear; and anoint thine eyes with eye-salve, that thou mayest see."

Behold,

Behold, then, two characteristics here described; the one self-sufficiency, and the other that to which a conceit of our own worth and attainments so naturally gives rise, indifference to the service of our Maker: and consider with yourselves, whether the conduct of the present age be not strongly marked with both. In the whole history of the human race was there ever a generation that treated past times with the overbearing insolence that the present does? If we listen to the swarm of writers with whose works so many presses daily teem, would they not fain persuade us, that they are the enlighteners of mankind, and that all who have gone before them were, in fact, the slaves of ignorance, superstition, or errour? and has not this malady spread like a gangrene? Is it not perceptible in the common conversation of the age? Has it not infected the language of the senate, the bar, and even of that where affectation should least appear, the pulpit? Nay, has it not descended to the artisan and the mechanick? who will tell you that the present are

are not like former times, when the people were unacquainted with their rights, but now they will think for themselves, being as able to do so as those above them? On questions of religion, indeed, our present more immediate concern, it seems to have shewn itself both earlier and stronger than on any other. One sect has long prevailed in Christendom, who having made an idol of their own reason, find neither the words of inspiration of sufficient authority, nor the wisdom of God wise enough for them. *No* authority is too high for them to attack, *no* doctrine too important for them to reject. Even the means by which God is pleased to reconcile the world to Himself, must be submitted to their judgement, and the operations of that eternal Spirit, who is above all, through all, and in all, must accord with their imaginations, and the nature of their Creatour be to be comprehended by these self-sufficient sophists, who think they have no need of either atonement or grace. The propagation of opinions like these, among a generation already thinking themselves

selves rich in knowledge, has proved like adding fuel to fire, and every petty disputant now thinks himself able to judge of the decisions of the wisest who went before him, and would have his rejection of their judgement be considered as a certain proof of the soundness of his own.

But while self-conceit has thus produced a rage for innovation in every branch in our own country, in what dreadful shapes has it shewn itself, what havock has it made in other parts of Christendom! There the pretences of instructing, improving, and exalting mankind to a degree which those of past ages never knew, hoped, or thought of, have affected the people like an intoxicating potion, and their leaders breaking down every ordinance that had been deemed necessary for the preservation of human society, destroying every thing beneficial, have opposed and exalted themselves above all that is called God, or that is worshipped, and discarding revelation, have endeavoured to obliterate from the minds

minds of men all recollection of their dependence on their Maker, by abolishing the observation of the sabbath, observed from the creation of the world in acknowledgement of it. And what is a novel occurrence among men, armed hosts have been marched from one sea to the other, not to plant a new religion among the nations, but to drive faith from the earth: while their commanders daringly vaunted their own apostacy and rebellion against Heaven, by shamelessly pretending to acknowledge the dissentient creeds of different countries, as long as such hypocrisy could forward their designs on those who dwell therein.

To lukewarmness in religion, to the decay of all sincere attachment to the faith, may the rapid progress of those pernicious opinions, of which such are the bitter fruits, be too in part ascribed; as well as that cold insensibility with which, for a long time, so many governments viewed their extensive diffusion. Although, indeed, the listlessness

ness which these betrayed, though by many ways loudly admonished of their danger, and the blindness with which so great a portion of several nations have rushed to their own destruction, should seem to indicate, that the threatening contained in the passage of the text is already executed on them, and that the Lord hath already spued them out of His mouth: while His judgements on them are proceeding in the manner thus foretold by the prophet, " Behold, the name of the Lord cometh from far, burning with His anger, and the burthen thereof is heavy: His lips are full of indignation, and His tongue as a devouring fire: and His breath as an overflowing stream shall reach to the midst of the neck, to sift the nations with the sieve of vanity: and there shall be a bridle in the jaws of the people causing them to err."

" Suppose ye, (said our blessed Lord to those that told Him of the Galileans, whose blood Pilate had mingled with their sacrifices) that these Galileans were sinners above all

all the Galileans, becaufe they fuffered fuch things? I tell you, Nay: but, except ye repent, ye fhall all likewife perifh." Thus teaching us to reafon from the divine judgements that overtake others, to the danger of our own ftate, from whom the fame fentence is withholden only by the forbearance of God. When, then, we fee " the whirlwind of the Lord going forth with fury," (Jer. xxxiv. 23.) and that " a continuing whirlwind," and have been warned, that " it fhall fall with pain upon the head of the wicked," Does it not become us to confider, whether we ourfelves be not in truth of that defcription? When, too, the portion of punifhment that has reached us does not exceed the meafure of rebuke and chaftifement, while on fo many others it has been extended even to deftruction, Does it not behove us to make ufe of the time granted us by the divine mercy, and examine how far we partake in that guilt which is menaced with overwhelming indignation from Him? " So, then, becaufe thou

thou art lukewarm, and neither cold nor hot, I will spue thee out of my mouth."

Now if we fairly confider how far we have manifefted this difpofition, fhall we not find that it has been long working among us: from thofe who have affected to confider religion as a mere inftrument of policy, contributing to the tranquillity and eafy government of the ftate, to thofe who have imagined all modes of faith equally acceptable in the fight of God, provided they are profeffed with equal fincerity? Shall we not find that it fhews itfelf in a lamentable and extenfive neglect of the means of religion? The fact itfelf cannot be difputed. Family devotion is fallen into I am afraid, I may fay, general difufe: the attendance in the affemblies of the church, even on the Lord's day, is extremely fmall in proportion to the number dwelling in the different parifhes, and what a ftill greater difparity is there between thofe who come to church, and the few, the very few, that are found willing to join in commemorating the death of our Saviour until His coming again! And can ye think this conduct is— Can ye venture to give to it the name of zealous? Be not deceived: our Lord requires it of us to seek the kingdom of God and His righteousness *before all* things. This ye know. Say, then, whether ye do not pursue the means of temporal prosperity, of worldly good, with more earnestness, with greater warmth, than ye thus cultivate the means of religion? For if ye do, your own hearts will convict you of want of zeal as to the latter; and " if our heart condemn us, God is greater than our heart, and knoweth all things."

The publick character of a country is so generally thought to be affected by the prevailing manners of its inhabitants, that we reason with confidence from the former to the latter: May we not thus then argue, that the neglect into which are fallen many salutary laws, enacted for the preservation of the morals of the people in this country, the general inattention of the magistrates

to

to the execution of such statutes, and to the whole of that portion of their duty, and the discouragement and opposition with which the few who would perform it meet, indicate a general indifference of the inhabitants of the land to the preservation of a conduct suitable to the profession of the Gospel, and that prophaneness and blasphemy, sabbath-breaking and drunkenness, impurity of every kind, and that potent enemy of every virtue, gaming, are deemed among us crimes of not sufficient magnitude to merit animadversion. When the legislature of a country is apprized that its former laws are either so fallen into disuse, or by the discovery of new evasions, are so eluded, as no longer to answer the purposes for which they were originally made, if there be any earnest desire, any real intention to effect those purposes, if there be any zeal, the laws deficient will be immediately re-enacted, or amended; and where such laws relate to the preservation of christianity among a people, their being permitted to become useless, is in itself no
weak

weak proof that the community in which they once were executed is become lukewarm in the faith of Christ. But should such legislature absolutely refuse (as has lately been the case among us) an application expressly made for the amendment of laws for the securing the honour due to God; What is this but saying, we will not that He should reign over us? And then, alas! unless humble acknowledgement, the sincerest repentance, and early amendment prevail, to have the provoked judgement averted, can shepherds like these expect a sentence less severe than that which the Lord pronounced against the husbandmen of His own vineyard, that " the kingdom of God shall be taken from them, and given to a nation bringing forth the fruits thereof?"

Again; it is far from consistent with zeal in the service of a king to suffer his subjects to be seduced from their allegiance by the propagators of doctrines contrary to his authority, a remark confirmed by the practice

practice of our own legiflature, which has enacted ftatutes for the repreffion of thofe who preach difaffection, or fpread fedition in the nation. But has the fame care been fhewn in the caufe of the King of kings? Has not, on the contrary, the circumfpection which our forefathers ufed on this point, been laid afide, and fome of the provifions which their wifdom made, been revoked with fcarcely the fhadow of a reafon, and a door been thus opened to the teachers of that corrupted church, from whofe abominations our anceftors were zealous to cleanfe, and to preferve their country? And have we not thus contradicted the warning voice which cries, " Come out of her my people, that ye be not partakers of her fins, and that ye receive not of her plagues;" and even at the time when her fins have reached unto Heaven, and God appears by the judgements that are now falling on the countries of her communion, to have remembered their iniquities, Have we not proclaimed, " Return to her ye who will, for no harm fhall happen unto you?" And can we

SERM. XV.

wonder if after this, something more than mere want of zeal in preserving the purity of the Gospel among us, the plagues poured upon her reach, in their effects, even to ourselves?

The affectation of generosity of mind, (termed in the spurious language of the present day, liberality of sentiment) superiour to that of former ages, manifested in this case, is, in fact, an instance of that self-conceit, by which our age is characterized in the prophecy before us. If ye listen to our professions, we possess more Christian charity, have juster notions of religion, and hold sounder maxims of policy, than the generations before us: yet attend to facts, and we have, in the first place, shewn our Christian charity, by proving ourselves much less solicitous about the future salvation of our people: in the second place, the juster notions of religion we possess, are manifested by our attending less to the only source of sure instruction in it, revelation, by our neglecting the means of it, it, and expofing ourfelves to be blown about by every wind of doctrine, and letting the influence of it appear lefs on our practice: and, laftly, the foundnefs of our policy is made known by our again introducing to our country, thofe through whom the liberty of it was before nearly overthrown, and opening a door to offences which we fee have produced confequences of the moft lamentable and fearful kind in various others. And now, arguing from thefe premifes, on the truth of which ye may yourfelves determine, which character is, in reality, moft applicable to us, that we give ourfelves in faying, we are rich and encreafed with goods, or that fupplied by the paffage of Scripture we are confidering, " Thou knoweft not that thou art wretched, and miferable, and poor, and blind, and naked."

In truth, nothing is more likely to lead either individuals or nations to think highly of themfelves than an encreafe of earthly treafures: the obfervation is in every body's mouth,

SERM. XV.

mouth, and general experience confirms it. When the land of Judah was replenished from the east, its inhabitants had the harp and the viol, the tabret and pipe, and wine in their feasts: but they regarded not the work of the Lord, neither considered the operation of His hands. Yet had they the writings of Moses which threatened them with all the curses written in his law, whenever they forsook the testimonies of the Lord their God: and the Lord, too, had begun to cut the neighbouring kingdom of Israel short for the transgressions committed in it. Thus, too, have we seen the wrath of God fall on the nations near us, while, by the passage of the text, and many others, we are warned of the evils that must overtake us, if we do not repent. The correction we at present feel has, in a manner that calls most loudly for our admiration and our gratitude, fallen principally on that of which we are proudest, which has contributed mostly to our corruption, and principally damped our zeal, I mean our wealth. As if the long-suffering of the Lord

Lord would kindly point out to us by this mean, how little that to which we are so much inclined to truſt, can help us in the day of wrath. And ſhall this kindneſs make no impreſſion on our hearts? Shall not theſe inſtances of His love induce us to ſtrive to make ourſelves more worthy of it? Shall not theſe fatherly rebukes and chaſtiſements make us zealous and repent?

The blindneſs which has, in part, happened unto us, and which prevents our ſeeing how miſerably we have departed from the line of conduct preſcribed by the Goſpel, can only be removed by the true light; And can we hope that that light will manifeſt Himſelf unto us, unleſs we *zealouſly* ſeek for His illumination? Do but, with the little ſtrength ye have yet remaining, apply yourſelves earneſtly to practiſe all which ye already know to be the duties of religion: give in reality that preference to the things belonging to the kingdom of God, which a very little conſideration will convince you is juſtly due unto them; and

be

be assured, that to the earnest prayer which forms part of those duties, ye will meet with such returns as will open your eyes to our real situation, not only in regard to the unrighteousness of our own behaviour, but in respect likewise to the urgent calls now made on us to repent without delay, because the kingdom of Heaven is at hand.

When our Lord rebuked the Jews because they could distinguish the signs of the weather, but were not able to discern those of the times, the period of the destruction of Jerusalem was not, I conceive there is reason to think, at many more years distance from that generation, than the time of His return to take vengeance on those who know not God, and obey not His Gospel, is from ourselves. I have already stated to you that the prophecy so descriptive of the period in which we live, is that which relates to the very last state of the church previous to that aweful event: and the great characteristick I have pointed out, lukewarmness in religion, is especially noticed

ticed by our blessed Saviour, in the account of the signs of His coming, recorded by St. Matthew; and encouragement not to give way to it, added to the mention of it; " And because iniquity shall abound, the love of many shall wax cold. But he that shall endure unto the end, the same shall be saved." While other symptoms of the end being near at hand encrease upon us. Of these it is ours to put one another in mind, and rouse each other to be zealous in preparing to meet our divine Master; both from the consideration that we must be left without excuse, if after such warnings of its approach that day overtake us unawares, and we be found drowned in the cares or pleasures of life, smiting our fellow-servants, or eating and drinking with the drunken: and from the glorious prospect of the honour and happiness that those will inherit, who resolutely adhering to the words of Christ, during the trials that remain to be undergone, shall either die in the Lord, or tarrying until He come, be of

Him

Him found watching, and made, according to His promise, rulers of all His goods.

In discharge, then, of this my duty, I have now declared unto you, brethren, that this is the last time, and as ye have heard that Antichrist should come, even now there not only are many Antichrists, but that power which the spirit of prophecy especially pointed out as Antichrist, and which is not to be finally destroyed until the coming of the Lord Himself, I mean, that of the pope of Rome, who, by calling himself the vicar of Christ, took to himself this title in one sense of it, as it belonged unto him in another, because he opposed the true doctrine of our Lord; this power, I say, has now continued very nearly the whole time expressly assigned to him: while such is the present situation of things, as to render it reasonable to suppose, that something very important in his history will very soon take place. Another power too, that of the Turkish empire, on the removal of which the last very few years of suffering will commence,

commence, seems to hold his present station at the will of two neighbouring monarchs more powerful than his self, and who too, may plead the example of their predecessours, for dividing neighbouring dominions between them: and whenever this power be removed, those days will actually begin that are shortened for the elect's sake; and, consequently, the sign of the Son of man very quickly appear in the clouds of Heaven. When then, He is, as it were, even at the doors, what counsel can we take but that of the text, " Be zealous, therefore, and repent?"

Let me then, in the last place, exhort, nay, let me beseech you, not to reject this counsel, as ye would wish for support under the encreasing afflictions of the present time, as ye would wish to avoid evils incomparably severer, and which must endure for ever and ever: as ye would wait without horrour for the appearance of your almighty Judge, and receive from Him crowns of glory and immortality. For if these considerations will not prevail with you, I have no more to add; but must conclude with the impressive words of Moses, "Behold, I have this day set life and death before you, therefore chuse life, that ye may live!"

SERMON XVI.

ON THE NATIVITY.

St. Luke II. 11.

For unto you is born this day in the city of David a Saviour, which is Christ the Lord.

THESE words contain what the heavenly Messenger announced to the shepherds, as " good tidings of great joy to all people." On what account they were so, I have before explained to you in a discourse on the predictions relating to the Messiah: and in that, too, I laid before you the characteristicks by which this great person might certainly be distinguished, whenever He should appear. However adapted,

SERM. XVI.

adapted, therefore, those points may seem to a discourse on this day, or how properly soever coming under the words of the text, I shall not now speak to them again, but make it my present business to enquire into the ground and meaning of the title of Christ here given to the Saviour, and into the relation indicated to subsist between Him and us, by the term Lord; and close my address to you with considering what obligations that relation confers on us.

Now the term Christ being, as is well known, a Greek word, equivalent to the Hebrew word Messiah, and both signifying anointed, it became particularly applicable to the Saviour, because He was to be invested with three offices, to each of which, under the law, admission was given by unction; those of priest, prophet, and king: and because, too, He was to receive an unction before unknown in the world, that of the Holy Ghost, which descended on Him in a bodily shape.

That

SERM. XVI.

That the priests were anointed to their office, we learn from the divine commandment to Moses, preserved in the fortieth chapter of the book of Exodus, which runs thus: " And thou shalt put upon Aaron the holy garments, and anoint him, and sanctify him; that he may minister unto me in the priest's office:" and that the Messiah was to bear this character, was foreshewn by the word of the Lord in the mouth of the psalmist; " The Lord hath sworn, and will not repent; thou art a priest for ever after the order of Melchisedeck." A point worthy of particular attention, because, as the apostle to the Hebrews argues, if perfection were by the Levitical priesthood, (under which the Israelites received the law) what further need was there that another priest should rise after the order of Melchisedeck, and not be called after the order of Aaron? For the priesthood being changed, there is made of necessity a change also of the law. And thus are we supplied from their own scriptures with a refutation of the Jews' conceit,

that

that their ceremonial law was not to be abrogated by the coming of Chrift. As long as the authority of that law continued, no one but a defcendant of Aaron could minifter in the prieft's office; and carefully did the individuals of the family preferve their genealogy; while the fate of Korah and his company held forth a moft awful warning, that no man who was not duely called, fhould prefume to take this miniftry to himfelf: but Chrift was announced as appointed to the priefthood, after an order in which there was no mention of father, or of mother, or of defcent; the miniftry of which was not confined to a particular people, but, like the falvation promifed by this High Prieft, to extend to the Gentiles, and reach unto the end of the earth. And as the prieft's office was to offer facrifice, and make interceffion and atonement for the people, entering once a year into the Holy of holies, for the performance of the moft folemn act of this laft, fo our bleffed Lord, having by one offering of Himfelf, perfected for ever them that are fanctified, entered

entered into the Heaven itself, where He liveth for ever to make intercession for us. Since, then, to the thoughtful son of Israel, there must have appeared in the sacrifices which were continually offered, in the blood of bulls and goats, no natural efficacy to take away sins, and yet he was sure that these offerings were not the offspring of human fancy, but the ordinances of divine wisdom, had it once been suggested to him, that the benefits attached to these were so merely on account of their relation to better things to come, Would he not with joy have received the explication, and gratefully viewed the beautiful correspondence between the emblematical institutions of the law, and the mercies of God, unveiled in the Gospel? Some such were found in the generation to whom Christ his self preached: and the prejudices of the present Jews will scarcely be met with so great promise of success in overcoming them, as with arguments drawn from the types of the Mosaic law: by such arguments we may triumphantly prove, that in Jesus these were fulfilled,

filled, and that He was ordained of God first, as there could be no remission without blood, to put away sin by His own blood, and then to appear in the presence of God for us, an High Priest for ever, after the order of Melchisedeck.

Of the introduction to the prophetick office by unction, an instance is preserved in the history of Elisha, whom Elijah was commanded to anoint to be prophet in his room; and as we find no other instance of the kind recorded, yet are told that a double portion of the Spirit rested on that prophet, we may well presume, that by this peculiar distinction, it was designed to mark him for a type of Christ. The designation of this great person Himself under that character, is contained in these words of the Lord to Moses, to be found in the eighteenth chapter of the book of Deuteronomy; " I will raise them up a prophet from among their brethren, like unto thee, and will put my words in His mouth; and He shall speak unto them all that I shall command him.

him. And it shall come to pass, that whosoever will not hearken unto my words which he shall speak in my name, I will require it of him."

Now the office of a prophet, ye know, was not confined to that to which we at present generally restrain our ideas of it, the foretelling of future events; but extended to interpreting the will of God to the people: he resolved their doubts, he reproved them for their transgressions, he delivered to them, in the name of the Lord, promises of future blessings on obedience, and denounced judgements to come: he was (according to that sublime description of his appointment given to the prophet Jeremiah) " set over the nations, and over the kingdoms, to root out, and to pull down, and to destroy, and to throw down, to build, and to plant." In these several particulars, therefore, did our Lord act; He explained the real meaning of the law and the prophets, and made known the whole will of His Father to the people: He declared

SERM. XVI.

clared the approach of an everlasting kingdom, into which the righteous should be admitted; and menaced utter destruction to those who would not receive His gospel. He foretold the overthrow of Jerusalem, the extirpation of all His enemies, and the establishment of His church, its continuance, spite of every opposition, and its final triumph. How greatly He resembled Moses in several particulars, I have already stated to you in a former discourse; and that He spake also in His Father's name. I shall here only notice a solemn declaration He made of this last, which was peculiarly calculated to call to the minds of His hearers this characteristick of that prophet that was to come into the world: it is in the two concluding verses of the twelfth chapter of St. John's gospel; " For I have not spoken of myself, but the Father which sent me; He gave me a commandment, what I should say, and what I should speak. Whatsoever I speak, therefore, even as the Father said unto me, so I speak." As He came not to condemn the world, but to save it, it, we read of but one act of severity during His whole ministry, and that was executed on a creature insensible to pain; the fig-tree, I mean, which He cursed for its barrenness, in significant allusion to the sentence gone forth against the ungrateful city that made no return for all that the divine husbandman had done unto it.

Further, too, as our Lord discharged the office of a prophet in all these particulars, so He demonstrated the justice of His own claim to the character by that incontrovertible proof which was laid down in the law, the completion of His words. The manner of His own death, the success of His gospel, the overthrow of the city and temple, the sufferings of His followers, and the history of His church, have all accorded with His predictions concerning them; and we challenge our adversaries to produce a single instance, in which what He hath really said, has not followed, nor come to pass, and when they do, we will acknowledge, that it was spoken presumptuously,

tuously, and that they need not be afraid of Him.

It is so well known, that the monarchs of Israel were wont to be anointed for their royal dignity, that it is needless to quote texts in confirmation of this point, but that Christ was to hold this office, we learn from the psalms and the prophets; " The kings of the earth (said David in spirit) have set themselves, and the rulers take counsel together against the Lord, and against His anointed—then shall He speak unto them in His wrath—yet have I set my king upon my holy hill of Zion." And in the thirteenth chapter of the prophet Jeremiah, " Behold the days come, saith the Lord, that I will raise unto David a righteous branch, and a king shall reign and prosper, and shall execute judgement and justice in the earth. In His days Judah shall be saved, and Israel shall dwell safely: and this is His name whereby He shall be called, The Lord our Righteousness." And Zechariah, in words exactly describing our Lord's

Lord's entrance into the holy city, "Rejoice greatly, O daughter of Zion; Shout, O daughter of Jerufalem: Behold thy King cometh unto thee: He is juft, and having falvation; lowly, and riding upon an afs, and upon a colt, the foal of an afs."

But here the prejudices of the Jews operate more powerfully than on any other part of the character of Jefus. Having, from their eagernefs to be delivered from the fervitude in which they had been fo long holden, formed to themfelves a notion that Meffiah the King was to appear from the firft in power and great majefty, and deliver them from all their enemies round about, they overlooked thofe prophecies which fpake of the intermediate ftate of humiliation, which defcribed Him as laying down His life for many, as ranfoming His people with His own blood, and through afflictions making His way to the glory that fhould follow. Hence the crofs became the great ftumbling-block; and we have been queftioned, How the dignity of
the

the Messiah was compatible with that? Yet were there not wanting ensigns of sovereignty not only in the authority with which He commanded the winds and the sea, and they obeyed Him; but when He ascended up on high, led captivity captive, and gave gifts unto men: for those gifts, the exercise of which his enemies did both see and hear, manifested the perfect truth of all the claims He had made to be the Christ, the Son of God, and consequently, the King of Israel.

Having thus investigated the several reasons for which the title of Christ was applied to our blessed Saviour, and shewn, that to Him it belongs in the triple character of priest, prophet, and king, it remains to consider the relation which subsists between Him and us, indicated by His being in the text denominated The Lord, and the obligations thence arising on ourselves.

Now the term Lord includes under it that absolute dominion which arises from property.

property. His we are, as originally by right of creation, so since by purchase, being bought with a price, that of His blood shed for our redemption. More particularly His we are by the Father's especial appointment, who hath made Him both Lord and Christ, and given Him all power in Heaven and in earth. It is in reference to this particular relation to us, that the apostle tells us, that there is, as one God, so one Lord, Jesus Christ: and by example as well as precept, hath taught us to look up to Him, as our immediate Protector and heavenly Master; and these several grounds of authority over us are all included in the declaration of God's Messenger in the text, That the Jesus, whose birth He then announced, was Christ, The Lord.

Now the light in which we are thus taught to consider our blessed Saviour, as our Master and our Owner, is not restrained to this world, but extends to that which is to come, wherein, having taken account of His servants, He will award each of them that
recom-

recompence for which his obedience or his disobedience, his fidelity or his faithlessness, manifested here shall call. What measure of obedience then, what degree of attention to His will is due to one whose authority over us is so justly founded, whose power is so unlimited? If He who endowed us with all our powers, require the service of them all, Is He demanding more than His own? And if, in some cases, He require us only not to employ them in the transgression of His law, yet have no attention paid to His call, must not those who thus refuse Him attention, be guilty of deep ingratitude? If He who willingly laid down His life to ransom us from the powers of darkness, command us to take up the cross and follow Him, and be ready to lose our lives too for His sake and the Gospel's, Is He demanding any return which His preceding kindness to us has not merited at our hands? If He, on whose word depend our present lot and our future sentence, warn us to shape our conduct, and regulate our conversation in this world, according to to directions He has left us, if His admonitions be not listened to, What can we expect from Him but the treatment due to idle and disobedient servants, the loss of His protection, and banishment from His household?

I can but think, that if Christians would take into consideration that connection which actually subsists between their divine Master and themselves, and duely ponder on it, no small alteration would be produced in their conduct; and instead of being carried away by the wildness of passion, or being lost in insensibility to every religious duty, they would from gratitude for all the great things He has done for them, for all the love He has shewn them, through fear of His almighty power, and His judgements extending to eternity, live in sobriety, and walk with circumspection: through sense of the high patronage with which they are blessed, be zealous in acting worthy of the vocation with which they are called, and fearful of forfeiting that rank to which His love

SERM. XVI.

love has given them the means of rifing: and really count all things but lofs for the excellency of the knowledge of Chrift Jefus their Lord: and therefore I would imprefs on your hearts, that the feftivals of the church fhould never be permitted to pafs without recalling to our minds thofe great inftances of divine love which are commemorated on them. That of the prefent feafon, the Son of God's coming into the world, that whofoever believeth in Him fhould not perifh, but have everlafting life, fhould turn our thoughts to the confideration of what a great difference there muft be between the condemnation from which we may be delivered, and the life we may obtain, that God fhould vouchfafe to fend fo great a perfon to enable us to avoid the one, and fecure the other? and of what converfation becomes thofe for whom Heaven hath fhewn fo much regard?

In times of feftivity, the heart and the tongue are both too apt to tranfgrefs the bounds of fobriety and temperance; the former,

former, elated with mirth, roves in its imaginations, and the latter rapidly pours forth of its abundance: many are the words then uttered which, in the moments of cool reflection, vex the mind, and bring remorse not only on account of the impolicy or folly of them, but from their immorality and impiety. It is not that the peril of falling into sin at these seasons proceeds from religion being an enemy to chearfulness, or well-regulated mirth, but that men laying aside that caution and restraint which our degeneracy ever needs, suffer their spirits to be so elated, and their passions so raised, that the bounds of truth and modesty are transgressed, and the dictates of reason gain no attention.

Such ye must be sensible, in various degrees, are the trespasses into which men do too often suffer themselves to be betrayed when met together for the purposes of merriment and feasting: and if it be with justice that that we lament the folly, and reprove the perverseness of those who, in any case, abuse

SERM. XVI.

the favours they receive, when bleſſings which flow more immediately from the providence of God, as His corn, His wine, and the companions He hath given us, are turned into occaſions of vice and immorality, were we to encreaſe the rigour of our rebukes in proportion to the ingratitude and madneſs of the miſconduct, language could hardly ſupply terms ſtrong enough to repreſent to the tranſgreſſors in this reſpect the vileneſs of their offence; eſpecially if ſuch tranſgreſſors are, at the time of their offending, celebrating a religious feſtival. We have no ground for joining in the joy of ſeaſons like the preſent but as Chriſtians: it is in them that we not only rejoice among ourſelves, but ought to aſſemble univerſally, and do ſo in greater numbers, to celebrate that inſtitution which our bleſſed Lord has left us in memory of Himſelf. Should we then change theſe ſacred ſeaſons into times of riot and licentiouſneſs? Is not this profaning rather than obſerving the feaſt of the Lord? If we obſerve them not, (and let it particularly be attended to that we do not obſerve

observe them as Christian festivals, unless we join in celebrating the supper of the Lord) we must be guilty of the most ungrateful insensibility of His inexpressible love to us: and if, in our observance of them, we copy not the examples of our earliest predecessors in christianity, but prefer rather that of the Gentiles in their idolatrous feasts, indulging in lasciviousness, lusts, excess of wine, revellings and banquetings, Is not this giving occasion to our adversaries to mock and blaspheme? What must enemies of the Gospel (the number of whom by no means decreases) think of a religion, for which the very disciples of it have so little respect, that even while commemorating the facts which passed at the time of its first introduction among men, they transgress its laws? How often has it been objected to the doctrine we profess, " Ye talk of its purity and its power, But where is the reformation it has brought about? Do we not see characters as dissolute and profligate in the higher, as idle, drunken, and dishonest in the lower ranks of Christians, as among those of any religion?" Let me, I beseech you, when next I hear such questions put, not be obliged to recur to the general answer, "Many are called, but few are chosen;" but enable me to glory at least in the instance of mine own household; and to say, on your part, that neither my teaching, nor your faith, hath been vain. Then may we have great boldness not only in the presence of our adversaries, but in the day of the Lord; together with rejoicing at His coming, Who having once appeared in humility to bear the sins of many, shall unto them that look for Him, quickly appear the second time unto salvation.

SERMON XVII.

ON THE CRUCIFIXION.

TITUS II. 14.

Who gave Himself for us that He might redeem us from all iniquity, and purify unto Himself a peculiar people, zealous of good works.

ST. PAUL, in his first epistle to Timothy, makes mention of some, who having put away a good conscience, had also made shipwreck of faith; which is (though it may be hoped not in a very high degree) yet it is in some measure, the case of all those who continue in the practice of sin; since the true faith of the Gospel, and the transgression of the commandments of God, are entirely

entirely inconsistent: for no man being willing to bring evil on himself; while those punishments with which the Gospel threatens the disobedient (be their excuse for their disobedience what it may) are sincerely believed, no man will subject himself to them; therefore when temptations arise, if the imaginary pleasures of sin allure, men immediately begin to look out for some hopes of escaping the penalty annexed, though they commit the crime; and this search is conducted in different methods, according to the difference of constitution, sense, and knowledge, that are to be found in men. Some of bold spirit, and a little information, (which is often worse than none) being on the one hand sensible, that if the Christian faith be well founded, there can be no hope for those who do not depart from iniquity, and, on the other, desirous of getting rid of all restraints on their pleasures at once, collect the several objections against the Gospel which have been raised by various infidels in several ages, and from the presumption that these may be just,

take

take courage to reject it as a forgery and an imposition, as a fable cunningly devised by man, and not a revelation worthy to proceed from God. Now of these men, we must at least say, that they appear to truely understand the terms of the Gospel-acceptance, and to honour the dispensation so far as to confess, that under it there is no security for vice. But there are others who equally backward to deny themselves the gratifications that are forbidden, yet either having the chief articles of the faith more deeply imprinted in their minds by education, or being of a less daring and more scrupulous disposition, do still continue to believe the truth of revelation in general; while they embrace opinions which are totally inconsistent with *that* of particular parts of it; in pursuance of which, they allow themselves with no apprehension of the wrath of God in practices that not only militate against some of His most express commands, but are diametrically opposite to the spirit of christianity; manifesting thereby, that though their faith continue

SERM.
XVII.
indeed with regard to the facts recorded in scripture, yet it is somewhat impaired with respect to the truth and importance of all its doctrines.

The consideration of the equal danger of these different errours will, I persuade myself, induce you, without further exhortation, to give me your attention while I set before you the doctrine of the text, which, if duely weighed, and faithfully retained, will be found a most desirable antidote to both.

The ends for which our blessed Saviour submitted to death were, as the apostle tells us, " to redeem us from all iniquity, and purify unto Himself a peculiar people, zealous of good works." And will the most confident of unbelievers presume to affirm, that this was a work so unworthy the Son of God to undertake, that the history of it is not to be believed? Was it needless? Or was it unimportant? Or does it manifest to us any attribute in the Deity, which

which the works of nature do not teach us
to acknowledge? Were not all men before
the coming of Christ in such a state that,
to use the language of scripture, they came
short of the glory of God? Were they not
ignorant of the dignity of their own nature, and of the purity and majesty of the
divine; and of the great and necessary
sanctions of religion? And did not their
ignorance, in these respects, lead whole nations into such practices, that, if permitted
to have continued, would have been a reproach to the Governour of the world, and
reflected disgrace on the Creatour of such
beings? But an end could not have been
put to these unless by either destroying
mankind, or instructing them, and improving their reason (which had already
shewn itself insufficient to guide them) in
such a manner, as might still leave them at
liberty to act as they would, while it gave
them power to discover and pursue that
course which was the right one. And
whether it were more worthy of God to
annihilate the race, or to afford them the
instruc-

SERM. instruction and assistance they needed, let
XVII. any man judge!

But farther; justice and mercy are to be equally ascribed to God; and they both shine forth with distinguished lustre in his natural government of the world: to vice and intemperance are annexed as their natural consequences, disease of body, and uneasiness of mind: virtue and sobriety, on the contrary, do produce peace within, and health and vigour without. And are not the glorious attributes I have mentioned, displayed too in the redemption of mankind by Christ? Consider the matter as stated in Scripture, first viewing the leading fact both as mentioned there, and confirmed by observation, " that man was created upright, a creature perfect in his kind, but did corrupt himself, and by doing what he was conscious he ought not to have done, acquired a degeneracy of nature. For God to have immediately interposed to have corrected this wilful depravity, without any satisfaction made on the part of man, would have

have been rewarding sin, and holding forth encouragement to His creatures to transgress His laws; it would have been acting totally inconsistent with justice, which demands as well that sin be punished, as that virtue be rewarded. The immediate destruction of the race was prevented by the divine wisdom and mercy, foreseeing, that if an offer of salvation was made on certain terms, *many* would *embrace* it, and recover to their own everlasting felicity, that perfection of nature, which they had first missed of by their father's fall, and *that* in the punishment of those who might reject this gracious offer, the justice of God would be still more manifest, since their ingratitude and perverseness in refusing the proffered mercy would render them both, in fact, and in the eyes of all rational beings, totally undeserving of further forbearance. Now could it be unworthy of the Son of God to take a principal part in a dispensation which, like this, was calculated to advance both the glory of His Father, and the happiness of His creatures, " wherein mercy and truth

truth would meet together, righteousness and peace would kiss each other?" If not, What have you to object to? Are you offended at the kindness which your Saviour has testified in doing so much for you? Or are you angry at the Gospel, because it sets forth, in a still brighter light, those very attributes which natural religion teaches us to ascribe to God? Because it affirms that He is of too pure eyes to behold iniquity; or that He is too just not to punish incorrigible sinners; or too good not to afford to those who will make use of them, opportunities and means of repentance and recovery?

But, perhaps, it is none of these singly, it is the whole of revelation together that you cannot digest; there is something mysterious and wonderful in it that you cannot account for, neither fully comprehend: And is it surprizing, that you cannot fathom the depth of the wisdom and goodness of God? It is as high as Heaven; What canst thou do? It is deeper than Hell; What canst thou

thou know? For once, then, lay aside the opinion of your own understanding being infinite! Pry not into secret things, for they belong unto the Lord! but be content to reason from what is already before you. That it was not inconsistent with the majesty of God to make such creatures as men, and provide for their temporal provision and comfort; your present existence, and all the enjoyments you have tasted, demonstrate; Why then deem it impossible, that, after He had made them, He should interpose to rescue them from the evils their own folly was bringing on them, and redeem them from all iniquity? This redemption is but an act of the same goodness that first gave you being; and its agreeableness to the character of God, is a pledge of the truth of Scripture in ascribing it to Him. The means made use of were, doubtlessly, surprizing; But who will be bold enough to say, that any others would have been adequate to the purpose? a wonderful and horrible thing had been committed; part of the universe had rebelled against their Creatour,

SERM. tour, and set his laws at nought. The eyes
XVII. of all rational beings, capable of viewing
and considering the dispensations of God,
which the Scripture informs us many are,
must have been immediately fixed on his
dealings in this case; and we may well
think, that the dispensation carried on to
remedy the evil in such a manner, as to
make His justice and mercy equally visible,
in His dealings with us His fallen creatures,
must have been miraculous on the whole;
while we may justly presume, too, that one
part of it would be, the purifying of those
who were willing, from the corruption they
had contracted, and restoring of them to
such a state that their existence should be
happy to themselves, and honourable to
God—In the words of the text, " Redeeming us from all iniquity, and purifying to Himself a peculiar people, zealous of good works."

But if the work of redemption be presumed to be adapted to the Son of God, in that it is the establishment of righteousness

and

and felicity, upon the ruins of sin and misery; How happens it, (it may be asked) that wickedness is still very prevalent in the world, when the knowledge of the Gospel is diffused more widely than ever? To this we have to answer, " That Christ came not to force, but to call sinners to repentance." To all who would listen to this call, He offered such spiritual assistance as should enable them to subdue their evil affections, and obtain habits of true virtue and holiness. Many have rejected this offer; many more have pretended to accept it, but proving unwilling to make the exertions required on their part, have received no benefit from it. Some few, however, in every age, have sincerely embraced it, and having passed through the proper season of trial, have been gradually transferred from hence, to a more happy state, there to wait God's appointed time, when the number of His elect being accomplished, He shall compleatly establish His kingdom of righteousness. Then shall be the full manifestation of the sons of God; and those who

SERM. XVII.

who have honeftly ufed the means of purification obtained by the death of Chrift, and turning from vice, have, through their own labour, made fuccefsful by His blefling on it, acquired a zeal for good works, fhall be declared his *peculiar people*.

How many there may be of thofe now working out their falvation on earth, we know not. It is evident, indeed, that there are among us, numbers who belong not to that flock, fince we can know them by the marks our Lord Himfelf hath left us, " their fruits." But whether all who do appear to the world to be zealous of good works are really fo, muft reft undetermined until the fecrets of all hearts be difclofed. And *thefe things* had the Gofpel taught us, that all mankind fhould have become holy through Chrift, might have been juftly objected to it; but that, on the contrary, though it inform all men how they may become fo, yet it always fpeaks of thofe who would behave like the true fervants of Jefus, as a fmall number in com-

comparison of those who would not, as— "a peculiar people."

To the description of which people, as given in the text and other parts of Scripture, I would particularly wish you to attend; for by seeing that the several declarations relating to them, all agree in giving them the same character, you will perceive that there is but one method of getting yourselves included in the number; which is a piece of knowledge not only important, but absolutely necessary: since there is no case in which the very common observation that we too easily credit, what we wish to be true, is more frequently verified than in this of religion; wherein men being desirous of obtaining salvation on the most easy terms they can, fondly receive those interpretations of particular passages that make the way to Heaven the shortest; and greedily listen to such teachers as, through folly, or impious craft, preach what is acceptable to their hearers, in lieu of what the Gospel contains.

SERM. XVII.

Against the infinuating doctrines of thefe falfe teachers, arm yourfelves with the following truths: "That if Chrift gave Himfelf for us, that He might redeem us from all iniquity; then ought every one who nameth the name of Chrift, to depart from evil; for he who does not, counteracts the purpofe for which the Redeemer died, and renders vain with refpect to himfelf the grace of God which hath appeared, teaching us, that denying ungodlinefs and worldly lufts, we fhould live foberly, righteoufly, and godly."

That while we are told, that Jefus died to purify to Himfelf a peculiar people, zealous of good works, we are alfo taught by the fame authority, that *that* purification is not brought about merely by the abfolute power of God operating on the feveral fubjects of it; but, by His grace, co-operating with their fincere and ftrenuous endeavours. For on what conditions did our Saviour promife the Comforter to His difciples? On that plainly of keeping His commandments..

" If

" If you love Me, said He, keep my commandments; and I will pray the Father, and He shall give you another comforter, that He may abide with you for ever." John xiv. 15. To whom did He promise to manifest Himself? and with whom said He, that His Father and He would make their abode, but with him who should keep His commandments? In what ground did He say, the seed of the word truely flourished, and brought forth fruit, but in *that* of a good and honest heart? *There may be*, who receive the word with joy, and keep it till temptation doth arise; *there may be*, who retain it a longer time, but in whom it is at length choaked with the cares, riches, or pleasures of this world; but *none of these* (I have the authority of our Lord for saying it) are of His peculiar people; *that* title belongs to those alone, who bring forth fruit with patience.

Therefore let not any man deceive you with vain words, or by persuading you to look within you for any fancied testimony of the spirit, induce you to overlook the apostolick rule, which is the only one that may be depended on, for determining whether you are the Lord's.—" That those who are Christ's have crucified the flesh, together with the affections and lusts thereof." To obtain for you the power to do this, was the end of Christ's submitting to death; the recollection of which, one might imagine, would raise in us the will likewise. Reflect only on the wonderful fact which we this day commemorate; the Son of God, after having condescended to take our nature on Him, stooping still further, and patiently passing through the lowest state of human misery!—Surely the different consequences of human conduct must be unspeakably important, that the knowledge of them should move so great a person as God to interpose, to turn us from the practice of sin to that of righteousness.—Whether we act according to, or against the dictates of our conscience; whether we obey or break the commandments of God; whether we walk in the narrow path of religion,

religion, and ramble in the broad ways of vice, can never be a matter of so slight moment as it is generally esteemed, since errours of little consequence would not have called down the Son of God from Heaven to rectify them. Much less now He has appeared, can it remain indifferent which course we pursue; that of righteousness or that of iniquity; whatever He hath established concerning the ends of each, must remain fixed and immutable; and in not listening to the instructions He hath left us concerning them, we shall acquire the accumulated guilt of despising the plainest lessons, given by the highest authority, manifested by the mean through which they were delivered to be of the utmost importance, and recommended by the compleatest evidence of the sincere love and good-will of Him who gave them; " For greater love than this hath no man, that a man should lay down his life for his friends."

The sum of the whole is this; that the Scriptures, in declaring the end of Christ's suffer-

sufferings to be that He might redeem us from all iniquity, and purify to Himself a peculiar people, zealous of good works, have given a reason for the wondrous fact which at once cancels all the objections of unbelievers, setting the divine wisdom, justice, and mercy, in the most glorious and amiable light; and at the same time takes every hope of the partaking of the benefits of His death, from all those who do not entirely forsake the works of sin which He came to destroy; and we, in pursuance of the apostolick direction, do continue to teach and remind you of these things; constantly exhorting you, that if ye do indeed, as ye profess to do, believe in God, ye be careful to maintain good works, looking for that blessed hope, and the glorious appearance of the Great God, and our Saviour Jesus Christ.

SERMON XVIII.

CONCLUDING DISCOURSE.

St. Luke xii. 32.

Fear not, little flock: for it is your Father's good pleasure to give you the kingdom.

"WHAT is man, that thou art mindful of him? or the son of man, that thou visitest him?" was the exclamation of one whose own history yields a remarkable instance of the free goodness of God; from following the sheep-folds had he been taken, and seated upon the throne of Israel; numerous were the dangers he encountered, and as numerous the deliverances he experienced. The dependence he felt on the divine providence, in his private fortunes,

SERM. XVIII.

fortunes, seems to have led him to extend his thoughts to the manner in which all mankind enjoy the blessings of God's government: and the great things done for this favoured race, struck him with admiration, but by no means shocked his faith; although on minds not so strong, and less informed, the very circumstance which calls the most earnestly for our gratitude and love, the unspeakable condescension of the Lord, sometimes raises doubts as to its own reality, and men are backward to believe, that such as they are, can be objects of so much regard to the Sovereign of the universe.

To Christians who have any misgivings of this kind, the text contains a satisfactory reply; because convinced of the divine authority of Him who spake the words, they can no more doubt, that it is the Father's good pleasure to give them the kingdom, than they can doubt of His power to perform what He wills. But the unbeliever may either except to the evidence given

given of its being the will of God, or say, that after all, the point itself is so incredible, that nothing but an immediate revelation to himself should convince him of its truth. Now to enable you to refute his objections, which ever of these grounds he takes, I shall make it the business of the present discourse, to apply so much of the evidence of religion as I have already laid before you, to his exceptions in the first case; and afterward suggest to you a full reply to what is advanced in the other.

In solution of the doubts, whether any attention is vouchsafed by the Deity to the human race in general, I first proved by appealing to your own feelings, that our Creatour hath implanted in our breasts a principle of religion in that indeterminate fear of some invisible Being which naturally arises in the human mind, and that, since a perfectly wise Being would never endow a creature with a faculty which had no object, the very existence of this fear within us is itself a proof, that He meant

the

the race should preserve a connection with Him by acts of devotion. In further reply to the same doubts, I next stated to you, that our own being, with such limited powers, and so precarious a mode of existence, affords a demonstration that the race received its beginning from One mightier than theirselves: and this constituting a proof from fact, that God did not think it unworthy of Him to make us, we may most confidently conclude, that after that He will not neglect creatures whom He has endowed with faculties to know, and serve Him.

In the next discourse, I laid before you the most manifest testimonies of the divine attention being extended to mankind, in the wonderful provision the Lord hath made for our support and comfort by the constitution of the material world; in which even many ill effects of our folly and ill conduct are provided against; these works evincing, that the Authour of them knew our necessities long before, and was able

and

and willing to furnish a supply for them: and I closed the consideration of this head of our heavenly Father's general care of our race, by stating to you some leading instances of the divine interposition in great political revolutions, and the proofs afforded by these, that the Lord hath not relinquished the government of the earth, but ruleth in the kingdom of men, putting down one, and setting up another, according to His good pleasure.

Having thus furnished you with answers to doubts that can be raised only by the actual Atheist, it became requisite next to consider, those which may be started against that exceeding greatness of God's love to men which the Gospel indicates. Here then it was shewn, that the more wonderful the facts taught us by revelation are, the more impressive is the evidence God hath been pleased to provide of the truth of that revelation, selecting, by a most signal dispensation, one particular people to be signs unto the world: to whose history the attention

tion of the other nations of the earth hath been called, after a remarkable manner, and to the continuance of whose singular state and wide dispersion we ourselves are eye witnesses. To this people were given statutes and a course of discipline, which rendered it more difficult for a mere pretender to inspiration to succeed among them than among the inhabitants of any other country on earth: and among them it was declared should appear that great Person, through whom all the sons of Adam might obtain deliverance from the evils brought upon the race by the disobedience of the first pair of it.

To this most important character were the expectations of that and other nations turned by a long course of predictions, which so specified all the particulars of His lineage, His birth, His wondrous acts, His extraordinary sufferings, and His singular triumph, that it was impossible the whole number of these should concur in any other than in Him, who was the real object of the

the prophecies: the nature of the falvation affirmed to be wrought by Him is fuch as never could have fuggefted itfelf to the mind of any one unacquainted with the true hiftory of mankind; and the remedies given for the corruption, the helps provided for the infirmities and wants of men, the manner in which their moft intimate defires are met, and in which their prefentiment and afpiration after immortality are accounted for, and objects worthy of their purfuit, and a fcene of action adequate to their powers are difclofed, and the prefent myfterious appearance of things explained, are fuch as could proceed only from the omnifcience and authority of the Maker and Sovereign of the world. Neither can the performance of fuch great things for mankind be accounted for but on the very motive againft which the objector points his doubt, the love of God to the works of His hands. That He fhould regard thefe is fo far from incredible, that it is hard to be believed He fhould do otherwife; and that the love of the Lord fhould move Him to

do

do those great things whereof we rejoice, the recollection of His abundant goodness and unlimited power may easily convince us: so that through these incontrovertible truths we regularly come to the conclusion, that " it may be His good pleasure to give us the kingdom;" and if it be so, Who shall counteract it?

The difficulty which men find in believing that the Almighty does so much for the human race, generally, perhaps, arises from their reasoning concerning His works, according to the notions they have formed from the deeds of men. The acts of benevolence which these do to any under their patronage, must be limited in proportion to the bounds of their own power; but His power being infinite, and His goodness perfect, His kindness needs to be restrained only by the capacity of those on whom it is conferred; and, consequently, it can never be in itself incredible, that He will give the kingdom to those who shall be found meet to partake of such an inheritance.

But

But by some, it is said, that many ages are past since this inheritance was promised, and still those who are said to be the heirs of it receive no distinguishing marks of being the peculiar favourites of Heaven; and hence arise other doubts as to the greatness of the divine attention to them. Now, surely, those who hold it incredible, that men should be objects of the regard of the Almighty, can hardly object, that if He deign to make them such, He keeps the times and seasons of conferring His blessings on them in His own power. The objection itself is, in reality, the same as that of the scoffers mentioned by St. Peter, "Where is the promise of His coming? for since the fathers fell asleep, all things continue as they were from the beginning of the creation:" and it merits the same answer, that the assertion it contains is not true, because even in the material world changes have happened, not only since the beginning, but since the publication of the Gospel; and how many more in the moral! How many of those facts have come to pass,

which

SERM. XVIII.

which our Lord and His prophets foretold should intervene between the age in which they lived, and the end of the world! And what is every accomplishment of a prediction relating to the church, but an additional proof that the fortunes of that church have been an object of His providence, Who can alone look with certainty into futurity? Behold, then, the symptoms required! To give a beginning to this kingdom among men, were, as I have shewn you, unnumbered miracles wrought; the power of death was vanquished, and heavenly gifts were given unto men; and to shew that it was the Father's good pleasure to give the kingdom to the little flock that then made its first appearance on the theatre of the world, it was by spiritual assistance only enabled to baffle all the attempts which the greatest earthly powers made to disperse and destroy it; and surviving all their efforts, gained possession of the imperial throne, receiving in this temporal a type of its everlasting triumph: and to preserve it from being overwhelmed by the most dangerous enemy

of

of all, profperity, were the corruptions confequent on that profperity foretold, and the ftruggles of thofe who would not join in thefe corruptions defcribed, and the judgements of God on fuch apoftacy predicted; by the whole of which is formed a courfe of prophecies reaching to that period when He who gave the promife of the text hath told us, He will return to perform it, and take His fervants to reign with Him.

Further, too, for the guidance of this flock while on earth, there have been given thofe laws which, in various other difcourfes, I have fet before you, and which prefcribe a conduct fuperior to all that the wifeft of legiflators, or of moral teachers, ever directed, or endeavoured to inculcate, and which is calculated to produce habits fuited to a more excellent ftate than that in which we now are fituated; and which habits we are told in the Scriptures that contain thofe laws, are required for the exprefs purpofe of rendering us fit to be admitted to that ftate.

SERM. XVIII.

When, then, such preparations have been made for the establishment of this kingdom, What want of significant signs that it is the Father's good pleasure to give it to this little flock? Who could thus openly take a people from the midst of all nations, and form them into a permanent society, on principles beneficial not only to themselves, but to all around them, and adapted to the everlasting promotion of peace and happiness, but the supreme Dispenser of every good and perfect gift? And is not His doing this, His calling them to a conduct and conversation which so often must expose them to ill usage from the wicked with whom they cannot but be mixed here, a sufficient indication that it is in a future state that the virtues to which they are here trained shall be exercised with fruit to themselves, and those who are found faithful in a little here, be there made rulers over much?

Having thus reminded you of the answers with which the discourses we have gone through

through have furnished you to the objections perverse or ignorant men may urge against the testimony we have of its being the good pleasure of God to exalt the faithful followers of Christ to never-fading crowns of glory, let us now consider the last plea in which the unbeliever endeavours to find refuge, that the point itself is so incredible, that nothing less than an immediate revelation to himself should convince him of its truth.

Now this plea would be less unreasonable, were it ours to determine after what manner God should make known His will to men; but even then it would proceed on a mere presumption, that of the insignificance of the human race in the eyes of their Creatour. For what is the ground of this imagination? here on earth all things are manifestly put in subjection under their feet: and what if there be innumerable worlds, inhabited by intelligent and moral beings, Will their number distract the attention, or exhaust the benevolence or power of the Lord; leaving but a little that He can do for men? Or, to come still nearer to the point, What is it that makes one creature of more importance in the sight of our common Maker than another? If there be any particular which does this, Is it not in the power of the Almighty to endow any species He pleases with it, and thus render them fit objects of His tender mercies? And on what ground will you presume to assert, that the sons of Adam have not been thus blessed? As far as human conjecture may venture to go, it should seem, that this consists in a capacity for happiness or misery, in the power of enjoyment or suffering: And who can say, that any beings possess this capacity in an higher degree than men do? At least the very same Scriptures that teach us, that our heavenly Father vouchsafes so much regard, inform us likewise, that we are made for everlasting duration, and, consequently, are capable of never-ceasing happiness or misery; and thus fully account for that tender concern which He

manifests

manifests for our inheriting the future blessings, and escaping the wrath to come.

SERM. XVIII.

Lastly, then, be it granted, that on the theatre of the universe this globe of ours may indeed seem to beings, reasoning as we do, of little comparative importance, yet since God seeth not as man seeth, neither worketh as man worketh, but manifests His glory by effecting His purposes by instruments weak in themselves, and apparently inadequate, may He not have chosen creatures, mean as we are, to serve Him in some grand dispensation, in which beings of higher rank, nay, the whole universe, are concerned; and if He has, all doubts arising from the presumed insignificance of the human species in itself, fall to the ground at once, since it is not for our sake, but His own glory, that He hath chosen us. Nor is it merely supposition that He has so. We are informed in the sacred writings, that superior beings are by no means unconcerned spectators of the work of human redemption. We are not only told

told by our blessed Saviour Himself, that there is rejoicing in Heaven over a sinner that repenteth, but by St. Peter, that angels desire to look into the dispensation; and that angels, authorities, and powers, are made subject unto Christ: and St. Paul asks his converts, " Know ye not that we shall judge the angels?" The analogy of the divine counsels in the Gospel, too, confirm the same thing. In the whole of that His strength was made perfect in weakness. From the lowest ranks of a nation at that time greatly despised, did the preachers go forth to preach to the nations the doctrine of Christ crucified; and, in the course of its promulgation, not many wise men after the flesh, not many mighty, not many noble were called; but God chose the foolish things of the world to confound the wise; and God chose the weak things of the world to confound the things which are mighty; and the base things of the world, and things which are despised, hath God chosen, and things which are not, to bring to nought things that are. That according as it is written,

written, " He that glorieth, let him glory in the Lord."

An attentive reader of the Holy Scriptures will find many paſſages corroborating, and explaining the idea I have now ſuggeſted to you, that the conſequences and effects of the Chriſtian diſpenſation are not reſtrained merely to the ſons of Adam. And what a ſcene is thus diſcloſed to the contemplative mind in the boundleſs extent, and ineſtimable importance of that ſcheme, in which a part is vouchſafed to every ſincere diſciple of the Goſpel! Often has it been argued, that we ſee but a portion of the government of God; and, indeed, an apoſtle tells us, (doubtleſsly intending ſomething more than to make a trite obſervation) that we know but in part. If, then, according to what I have now ſtated, we have been made by God to ſhew forth His praiſe on a more extended theatre than the globe on which we ourſelves dwell, the importance of our deſignation will ſolve many difficulties, and clear

SERM. clear many doubts, which men of partial
XVIII. enquiry are apt to start.

In the first place, the faith of such need be no longer shocked at measures so great and extensive having been taken to call the attention of men to the truths of religion. For as when we learn, that the people of Israel were, from the first, appointed to be the instruments of the salvation of God to the ends of the earth, we no longer find it difficult to account for the share of the divine patronage which they have enjoyed; when, according to the phrase of Scripture, He instructed them by His prophets, rising up early, and teaching them, so shall we no longer be surprized at the signal means used for the instruction of the human race in general, when we are informed, that from them are to be selected a chosen few to be exalted to a station conspicuous in the eyes of all created beings.

Neither will the greatness of the Mediatour be a stumbling-block on account of the

mean-

meanness of the race for whom He condescended to submit to death, if it be considered, that the consequences of this astonishing instance of humility and love may extend throughout the universe; and as, although He was crucified by the Jews, He died not for that nation only, but that also He might gather together in one the children of God that were scattered abroad; so although He took not on Him the nature of angels, but that of men, the glory of His exaltation may be felt by all the heavenly host.

Again; that which is in truth much the most extensive cause of offence, the purity of the laws, and the integrity of the morality of the Gospel, appear in this view of things to be matter of absolute necessity: for how should those who are not practised in self-command be fit to be entrusted with charges of importance. The question is that of our Lord Himself; " He that is faithful in that which is least, is faithful also in much; and he that is unjust in the least,

SERM. least, is unjust also in much. If, there-
XVIII. fore, ye have not been faithful in the un-
righteous manner, who will commit to your
trust the true riches? And if ye have not
been faithful in that which is another man's,
Who shall give you that which is your
own?" The abuse or neglect of wealth,
opportunities and faculties with which we
are now entrusted, manifestly indicate, that
to consign to us more important trusts,
would be the dictate of neither wisdom nor
justice; and therefore are we exhorted so
earnestly to live soberly, righteously, and
godly in this present world. To the
thoughtless lovers of it, indeed, these admonitions seem harsh, and being accustomed
to estimate the guilt of transgressions merely
by what others suffer through them, the
pernicious and destructive effects of the
personal vices are overlooked by them: yet
do but once seriously reflect, how totally
unfit those who have accustomed themselves
to make our heavenly Father's precepts of
righteousness give way to their passions or
their fancies, are to be advanced to stations

of

of higher honour, and of greater truſt, and you will ſee a moral impoſſibility, that thoſe who have paſſed their lives here in the ſervice of ſin or folly, ſhould ſhine as the ſervants of God hereafter: and if this high prize of our calling may be loſt through the tranſient gratifications of our bodily appetites, or of our corrupt inclinations of mind, through habits of intemperance or riot, of luxury or diſſipation, How inexpreſſibly important, how worthy of the moſt anxious attention, are thoſe leſſons which direct us to conſider theſe as enemies to our future glory and happineſs, and to avoid them! And how truely do they manifeſt themſelves to be the very dictates we might expect from Him, Who would that no man ſhould periſh, but that all ſhould come to eternal life!

Under this view, how are the trials we here meet with dignified, and how truely wiſe, juſt, and kind, appear the exhortations given us to fight the good fight, and bear hardſhip like good ſoldiers of Chriſt, that we may hereafter be crowned: and when such crowns are certainly laid up for them, how reasonably may the faithful followers of the Son of God deem all their sufferings in this life not worthy to be compared with the glory which shall hereafter be revealed in them. As, on the other hand, how severe will be the remorse, how bitter the anguish of those, who in that day shall find, that they are cut off from all inheritance among the people of God! This consideration is of itself, perhaps, sufficient to clear all doubts about the intenseness of the torments of the damned, without taking into the account the additional punishments which may be justly heaped on them, for their daring rebellion against their Creatour, and their ungrateful rejection of His proffered mercies. While the having secured a contrary lot for ever and ever must as naturally excite in the breasts of all, who receive a favourable sentence from the God of their salvation, a degree of rejoicing, and a permanency of happiness, by no means too highly described by any

any of the emblematical descriptions I have SERM. from the Holy Scriptures set before you, of XVIII. the joys of the blessed hereafter.

What then remains, but to exhort and to beseech you all, as partakers of this heavenly calling, not to think scorn of the proffered inheritance, or, like Esau, profanely sell your birth-right for a mess of pottage: for to you belongs the assurance of the text, and to as many both near and afar off as the Lord our God shall call. True it is, that in comparison with the multitude to which it has been extended, few have obeyed this calling; and even against this little flock the most vehement and ceaseless opposition has been made by the children of the world, and the powers of darkness: but the effect of this opposition hath been only to manifest which are the true, which the pretended disciple of Christ, to separate the wheat from the chaff, to try the elect as the gold is tried, in the fire, and to confirm the assurance of the text, that it is the Father's good pleasure

to

to give them the kingdom, by the pledge of this which His church has received in the never-failing protection and support vouchsafed unto it against all its enemies, and under all its trials; until, in the present age, that succession of signs which its divine Master was pleased previously to mark as symptoms of His return to take account of His servants, being nearly run out, the coming of our Lord approaches fast, and He is now (almost without a metaphor) even at the doors.

What manner of men, then, does it become us to be in all our conversation? Shall we, conforming ourselves to the fashion of the world, spend our time in rioting and drunkenness, in chambering and wantonness, in strife and envying; or putting on the Lord Jesus Christ, make not provision for the flesh to fulfil the lusts of that; but be like servants waiting for their Lord?

By thus delivering you a word of exhortation every Lord's day, I have so far endeavoured

deavoured to get myself numbered among those who shall be found not eating and drinking with the drunken, or beating the man-servants and maid-servants, but giving them their meat in due season; if ye will not receive, and duely use this spiritual food, your future and everlasting portion must be with the unbelievers; but if we all honestly unite in hearing the word, and keeping it, then at whatever hour the Lord returns, we shall be found watching; and for our brief sufferings, our trifling labour here, be recompensed with that inestimable sentence, " Come ye blessed of my Father, inherit the kingdom prepared for you from the foundation of the world."

FINIS.

www.ingramcontent.com/pod-product-compliance
Lightning Source LLC
Chambersburg PA
CBHW022334230426
43664CB00040B/604